Hope

Jeremiah Burroughs

Edited by Don Kistler

Soli Deo Gloria Publications

An imprint of Reformation Heritage Books

Grand Rapids, Michigan

Soli Deo Gloria Publications
An imprint of Reformation Heritage Books
3070 29th St. SE
Grand Rapids, MI 49512
616-977-0889
orders@heritagebooks.org
www.heritagebooks.org

First published as *The Tenth Book of Mr. Jeremiah Burroughes, Being a Treatise of Hope* (London, 1660).

Paperback edition published 2025

ISBN 979-8-88686-193-8

Printed in the United States of America
25 26 27 28 29 30/10 9 8 7 6 5 4 3 2 1

The Library of Congress has catalogued the hardcover edition as follows:

Burroughs, Jeremiah, 1599-1646.
Hope / by Jeremiah Burroughs ; edited by Don Kistler.
    p. cm.
Rev. ed. of: The tenth book of Mr. Jeremiah Burroughes.
    ISBN 1-57358-171-2 (alk. paper)
1. Hope-Religious aspects-Christianity. I. Kistler, Don. II. Burroughs,
    Jeremiah, 1599-1646. Tenth book of Mr. Jeremiah Burroughes. III. Title.
    BV4638.B88 2005
    234'.25-dc22
                                                      2005006779

Contents

Contents

Appendix

The Misery of Those Who Have Their Portion in This Life

Doctrine 1: There is a generation of men to whom God gives some outward good things for a while, but these are all that they are ever likely to have.

Doctrine 2: God's saints desire to be delivered from such kinds of men.

Chapter 1

The Coherence, the Scope, and the
Meaning of the Words

"And every man that hath this hope in Him purifieth
himself even as He is pure." 1 John 3:3

In the beginning of this chapter, the blessed state of
the saints of the most High God is proclaimed before
all the world: "Behold, what manner of love the Father
hath bestowed upon us!" We may well, with a kind of as-
tonishment and amazedness of spirit, admire this; but
the eloquence of men and angels is not able fully and
effectually to express it. We must be in heaven for some
time before we can take a due survey of all the dimen-
sions of this eternal fatherly love of God in Christ to
His adopted ones—"that we should be called the sons
of God"—that we wretched, base, vile sinners; that we,
not angels, should be called not servants, not friends
only, but that we should be called the sons of God; even
we who were the children of the devil, as firebrands of
hell in ourselves; that we should not only be plucked
out of the fire, but be called the sons of God, not only
be sons, but this should be made known that we should
be called the sons of God; this excellent and blessed
state of ours is spiritual, and is hidden from the world.
The world does not know us, and good reason, for it
does not know Him; the world does not know our
Father, it does not know Christ, and therefore we cannot marvel that they do not know us, nor know the
blessed condition we are in in being the sons of God.

Unknown princes are not respected.

The truth is, we know but very little ourselves of the blessedness of this condition. The happiness of the saints is a marvelous, secret, and hidden thing; but now that we are the sons of God, we know this much, that we are so, and yet it does not appear what we shall be. We are now so, yet, though we are now sons, we expect manifestations of greater and more glorious things than yet appear. We have the foundation of abundance of glory laid in, but we are sons; though we do not have our inheritance, yet it does not appear what we shall be. We now are in afflictions, and little difference appears between us and the men of the world; but we know that when He shall appear we shall be like Him. We are certain there is a time coming when God intends to let Himself out fully to His creatures; we have a little now that sweetens our hearts, and enables us to rejoice in afflictions and tribulations, but there is a time drawing near when He shall appear, when our blessed Savior shall come again and appear in glory, and these eyes of ours shall see Him—and when He shall appear, we shall be made like Him.

We have great things in hand, but greater things in hope; much in possession, but more in reversion. Let this comfort us against the contempts cast upon us by the world, which is blind and beside itself in the point of salvation. We are at present poor and mean, contemptible and sinful, the off-scouring of all things; but all sin shall be done away. These very bodies of clay that we carry about us shall be made like His glorious body, and our spirits likewise shall have the image of the Father fully resplendent in us. We shall be in such a condition as is fit for the appearing of our Husband, Jesus Christ; fit for enjoyment of communion with Him, to stand forever before Him, for we shall be like Him, and we shall see Him as He is. We see Him now but through a glass, dimly through the creature, through a lattice, through His ordinances, as an old man through spectacles, as a weak eye looks upon the sun; but in heaven we shall see Him as He is, so far as a blessed creature is capable of that blissful vision. Then we shall see Him face to face; we shall see Him even as He is. In the meantime, while this glory of God shall appear, we have the grace of hope put into our hearts; we wait for the time; we expect when this time shall come, and we rejoice with joy unspeakable and glorious when this shall be. Here is the hope of the saints, that such a time is coming.

Now what will this glorious hope do of such glorious things? The beatific vision of Jesus Christ, and being made like Him in glory, what will the hope of this do in the heart? "Every man who hath this hope in Him purifieth himself, even as He is pure." Once the Lord has raised such a hope as this is in the heart of a sinner, it will do mighty things there; it will cleanse the heart, purge it from the filth of sin, purify the heart even as Jesus Christ is pure, whom we hope thus to see, and to be made like. This hope of being made like Christ hereafter does, in some measure, make us like Him for the present. We hope that we shall see Him and be like Him, for "every man that hath this hope in Him purifieth himself, even as He is pure."

"Every man," not only eminent Christians, not only those who have great abilities and much grace do it, but every man, every soul. The faith of the weakest is of the same nature as the faith of the strongest, and has the same privileges in divers particulars. And so we have here in the text that the hope of the weakest is of the same nature as the hope of the strongest, for "every man who hath this hope." It is impossible that this hope can come into the heart of a sinner without it working out of his heart the love of his sins. This is true of every man who has this hope.

"This hope," it is as if the apostle should say, "There is a base, refuse hope in the world that will do nothing in the soul; but he who has this hope, this choice hope (as it is said of faith, that it is the faith of God's elect, so he who has this hope) has the hope of God's elect.

"This hope" either notes the choiceness and excellency of the hope, or else it means the hope that has such a glorious object as this hope has; this supernatural hope that has a supernatural object, the hope that enables the soul to hope for such great and glorious things. The men of the world have their hopes. One man hopes to increase his estate and grow rich; he has a fair way of trading; he hopes for a good voyage, and makes account that if such things return safely home, he must be thus enriched. Another hopes to get a good place; another hopes that upon the death of such a friend he shall get thus and thus. There are a great many hopes in the world, but "he who has *this* hope," says the apostle. The hopes of the saints are pitched higher than the hopes of the men of the world. They are raised up to high and glorious things, even to the appearing of Jesus Christ, to seeing Him as He is, and being made like unto Him—he who has *this* hope.

He who has this hope in Him purifies himself. Note that the word is "purifies," not "sanctifies." The difference in these words is this: to sanctify belongs to God Himself, to Christ. Christ says that He sanctifies Himself, and God is holy and pure; but this word denotes such a kind of sanctifying as implies a defilement. He purifies himself, cleanses himself from the filthiness of sin that is in him. When this hope comes into the heart, it finds a great deal of filth of sin in the inward man; but it is never at rest and quiet till it gets the filth of sin purged out, and that which he does, he does to purpose. This hope will not only keep a man from the gross and vile sins of the world, but it will purify the heart within. He purifies himself as Christ is pure. He makes Jesus Christ to be his pattern, to cleanse and purify his heart by. He is not satisfied until he gets to be like Jesus Christ, that immaculate Lamb of God, as *He* is pure. He reasons thus with himself: "What, do I expect to see Christ, and to be made glorious like Jesus Christ hereafter? Then let me make Christ to be my pattern now, to be as like Him as ever I can for the present."

He "who hath this hope in Him purifieth himself, even as He is pure." That is a true hope that runs out into holiness; faith and hope purge and work a suitableness in the soul to the things believed and hoped for. This is the true scope of the words, and the spiritual meaning of them.

Three things are remarkable in these words, and I shall make a doctrine from each.

Chapter 2

Three Doctrines Raised and a Description of Hope

The subject: every man who has this hope in him.
The act, or what he does: he purifies himself.
The pattern: as He is pure.
The doctrinal points are these:
1. Every man who is a child of God is a man of hope.
2. Where this hope is, it will purge the heart.
3. This hope causes such a purging as aims at the very purity of Jesus Christ. He purifies himself even as Christ Himself is pure.

The two latter ones are the chief doctrines that the apostle aims at here in speaking of this hope, yet I shall treat all three in order, beginning with the first point, which is intended likewise fully in the words, "every man that hath this hope." Every man who is a child of God is a man of hopes; he is born to great hopes, and he serves God for the present upon hopes of what he shall have. God has in His service two sorts of servants, as men have. Men have servants, some who they hire by the day. They have their day's wages after they have done their work, and all they can expect from their masters is to be paid for their work. You have other servants who serve great men and princes, who have nothing but meat and drink to serve them for a while. They are not hired servants for so much a year, but they serve in expectation and hope when such places fall that they shall be preferred to them. They are content to go on and serve many years, if they may but subsist in the hope of the favor of the prince or the nobleman to have such places when they fall.

In just this manner God has these two sorts of servants. There are many people who serve God, that is, do many outward good things for the present, but all that they have is but as a man's day's labor. They have their wages, their penny. God gives them outward prosperity, and many comforts in this world, and they aim at no higher things from God but that they may have their estates and live in some rank and fashion in the world; they look at such things. Many aim at credit and esteem. Why is it that they are forward in the profession of religion but for esteem and credit, for by ends, and God lets them have it. This is their wages, and all that ever they are likely to have from God.

But there are others who serve God, and they are willing to spend their strength and all that they have, are, or can do for God, and leave it to God to do with them what He will do. Others indent with God that they must have such esteem, credit, and estates.

"Nay," says a gracious heart, "Lord, as for these things, do with me what Thou wilt. I'll serve Thee as long as I have life and strength. Thou shalt have the glory of all. I'll do it upon Thy bare Word, what Thou hast promised for the life that is to come, merely upon the hope of what glory Thou has revealed in Thy Word for Thy saints. That shall be enough to me, though I never see a good day in the world in respect of my outward comforts; though the men of the world should use me against common sense and reason, and treat me ever so vile here, it's no great matter. I do not serve Thee for wages here; that which I serve Thee for is in hopes of what is a coming hereafter, and that wage is not a servile thing."

You never find in Scripture a hypocrite described as serving God out of hopes of heaven. We have no such character for a hypocrite indeed, but he looks for his reward here. So a hypocrite may be described. But if a man has an eye to the recompense of reward that shall be hereafter, it is grace that enables the soul to do this.

In opening this point, two things are necessary:

First, it will be very useful to open somewhat to you what this hope is. What is this hope of the saints?

Second, it will be useful to give you evidences that indeed they are men of hopes, and then briefly to apply it.

For the opening, as I did before of faith, so now what hope is. I may describe it thus: Hope is a grace wrought in the heart by the power of the Holy Spirit, whereby the soul quietly waits for, and expects the future good that God has promised in the covenant of grace, though there are many difficulties in the way to hinder the accomplishment of it. That is the nature of hope.

Chapter 3

Hope is Wrought by the Holy Spirit

The efficient cause of this grace (as others) is the Holy Spirit. Hope is a grace wrought by the power of the Holy Spirit. And I name it the rather because the hopes of most people in the world are the slightest and vainest things that can be, and there is no need of any great power of the Holy Spirit to raise such hopes as these are in their hearts. Their hopes are merely slight kinds of opinions that they have; they know not to the contrary but, it may be, God may be merciful to them. But mark what the Scripture says of the hopes of the saints in Romans 15:13: "Now the God of hope fill you with all joy and peace in believing, that ye may abound in hope through the power of the Holy Ghost."

First, God is called the God of hope. There is nothing that is an excellent grace but it gives God a title. Here He is "the God of hope." Surely God would not take this title to Himself unless it has a great deal of excellence in it. God accounts it His glory that He works such an excellent grace in the hearts of the saints (Romans 15:13). I appeal to your conscience, are your hopes such hopes as hold forth the glory of God in them? Are they such hopes that God Himself may glory that ever He raised such hopes in your hearts?

Certainly there's no piece of work that any of you do that you would hold forth to the world to glory in it, but you would suppose there were some great excellence in that piece of work. If a man should do a piece of work, and hold it forth to all the world, saying, "Let all the world see what I am able to do," and you would have the title of it. Such a man who did such a work, who made such a ship, as many shipwrights do who make very useful, gallant vessels, they would be glad to have their names transferred on them so that they may be known by such a name: "Such a man was the master builder of this ship, that frigate."

So the hopes in the hearts of the saints have such a great deal of excellency in them that God will have His name transferred upon them, and will be called the God of their hope. The truth is, when you speak of heaven, happiness, and eternal life, and ask what you think shall become of you, you hope it shall be well with you. Hope, if it is of the right stamp, the true grace of hope that is in the saints, is such a grace that the Lord accounts it His glory that His infinite power was able to raise such a grace in your heart. Considering what a desperate condition sin has brought the creature into, the infinite distance that sin had made between God and the creature, and the gulf that sin plunged the creature into, I say, it is a great part of the glory of God that He will glory to all eternity that He could raise up true hope in the heart of such a sinner to hope for such glorious things as indeed He has propounded in His Word to the sinner.

He is the God of hope and not only does God have His title from it, but it is here, through the power of the blessed Spirit, that your hope may abound through the power of the Holy Spirit; not only that you might have the Holy Spirit work hope in your hearts, but that it is the power of the Holy Spirit. There is a great emphasis in that, as if God had said that the Holy Spirit has raised hope in your hearts, and it could be raised by no other means in the world. That is certain, if it is the hope by which you shall be saved, that hope that will not fail to bring you to heaven. It is such a hope that all the angels in heaven, and all the men in the world, would not be able to raise in your hearts; only the Holy Spirit coming into your hearts raised this hope. Many who have vain and slight spirits, who know little of God and the breach that is between God and them by sin, think it the least thing in the world to hope. What, will you not hope in God's mercies? But that soul that finds the burden of sin upon it finds it the greatest thing in the world to hope, and it finds that no creature is able to raise hope in the soul. The minister comes and speaks excellent things, but alas, he does not raise hope; but the Holy Spirit must come and put forth His power to raise hope in the heart of a sinner who knows his sin and is made sensible of the weight and burden of it.

Thus it is a grace wrought by the Holy Spirit. These things describe it: The efficient cause of hope, the objects of hope, the acts of hope, and the grounds of hope. These are the four main things. The first I opened, the other three follow.

Chapter 4

The Object of Hope

The object of hope is some good, some future good, a supernatural good, and a difficult good; and therefore hope is compared to a helmet and to an anchor.

The object of hope is all the good, future good, promised in the covenant of grace and yet not fulfilled, but has many difficulties to hinder the fulfilling of it.

First, the object of it is that which is good; for if it is that which is evil, then we fear it, not hope for it.

Second, it is a future good thing. So the apostle says in Romans 8 that if we see a thing we do not hope for it, but that which we do not see, that we hope for.

Third, the object of the hopes of the saints is a supernatural good. Objects distinguish virtues, both moral virtues as well as theological ones too. Here the object is a supernatural good, and that distinguishes it from all the hopes of the world, from those who make the creature their hopes; but the hope of the saints is the fulfilling of all the good that is promised in the covenant of grace that yet is unfulfilled, all mercies that the soul or body stands in need of for this world and for the world to come. But that special object of this hope are the glorious things that God has promised in His blessed covenant to be fulfilled in the world to come; those things that are the most above sense and above man's reason are the objects of this hope: the appearing of Jesus Christ, seeing Him, being made like Him, and enjoying eternal communion with Him.

Fourth, this object is an object of hope that has a

difficulty, for so those who speak of the nature of hope make it to be not only *bonum, futurum,* a good thing, but a future good thing; but there is another thing, and that is a difficult thing; for a man does not hope for that which will come easily. For instance, when we go to bed, we do not hope that the sun will rise in the morning; or when we put a thing on the fire, we do not hope it will grow hot, because that has no difficulty in it. But when a thing has a difficulty, in that many things will hinder the accomplishment of it, then we say that we hope. When you send your ships to sea, you hope for a good return; there may be a great many difficulties in the way, but you look beyond those difficulties and hope for a good voyage.

So the object of hope is a good that has some kind of difficulty in it. The saints hope for salvation, mercy, life, and glory; but if they look into themselves, they see an abundance of things that might cross the good that they hope for. When they look upon the abundance of sin in their hearts that makes such a distance between God and them, that is so opposite unto God; when they consider the little service that they do to God, and the great dishonor that God has from them; when they consider how the promises are deferred that God has made, yea, when things seem to work contrary to the promises that are made, that is the usual way of God, that in His outward dispensations towards His people He seems to go quite contrary to what He has promised. Now this would tempt the soul to despair, and think, "Certainly, whatsoever God has promised, can it be fulfilled when things go so cross and contrary?"

Reason says it will not be; sense says it cannot be. Aye, but hope will then wait; hope will break through a great many difficulties and yet wait, notwithstanding that the things are not accomplished. Reason and sense say, "How is it possible that such a lump of filth and sin should stand before the face of the infinite God with joy, when as Jesus Christ shall appear with His holy angels, and God shall appear in the infiniteness of His holiness and justice, that such a poor wretch as I am should stand before Jesus Christ and His holy angels, and look upon His face with joy; that this body of mine that has been such an instrument of sin should be made like the body of Jesus Christ; that this poor soul of mine, so full of darkness and sinfulness, should enjoy eternal communion with Father, Son, and Holy Spirit—how can these things be?"

Now the grace of hope carries through all these difficulties. "I find God's ways towards me to be as if He were an enemy; yea, I pray to Him and He does not hear me. I am still in the dark and the terrors of the Almighty stick in my soul. Shall I ever come to enjoy His presence, and be partaker of all those glorious things that I have heard that the saints shall be partakers of in heaven?" These things make the object that the saints hope works upon to be a very hard, very difficult thing. And here's the use of hope, that when things appear to be very difficult, yet then hope will wait, will hold still. Therefore you find in Scripture that hope is compared to two things, a helmet and an anchor.

Hope is compared to a helmet in Ephesians 6, where it is called "the helmet of salvation," that is, the hope of salvation; that's the meaning. The helmet of salvation is the hope that you have of salvation; that is to be your helmet. Now what's the use of a helmet but to defend the head when we are in the midst of our enemies clashing their swords about our ears, to hold up the helmet and keep the head? So when a child of God is in the world, and meets with a great deal of opposition, and much evil that would discourage his heart, that would strike him at the very head, then he holds forth the hope of salvation as a helmet; and that will serve him; that will secure his head. It may be that his legs, or some other parts, may be touched, but the helmet of salvation will secure his head and keep him alive. Thus it is when we meet with opposition at hand.

But there are dangers at sea as well as by land; and that you have in Hebrews 6:19, where hope is compared to an anchor. This hope we have as an anchor of the soul, both sure and steadfast, and which enters into that which is within the veil. This is the elegant similitude for the expression of the hope of the people of God by which those who are seamen especially may learn very much, and especially the Holy Spirit speaking by their own art and skill. They know what the use of an anchor is when they are at sea. If they did not have a good strong anchor, what would they do? They do not have so much need of it in calm weather; they do not care so much for a fair, painted anchor; if they cast their anchor when the winds and tempests come, and the rocks are hard by them, so that if the anchor fails them, they are split upon the rocks or run into the sands. Then, oh, how they esteem a good anchor at such a time, and see cause to bless God for the use of it. Thus Christians should expect (for they are mariners, all Christians are in the world as the mariners in the sea), though they have calms sometimes, yet they are to expect tempests and storms. Temptations and oppositions will be ready to split their souls upon the rocks or run them upon the sands.

Now in times of greatest opposition, and of the greatest temptations, there a Christian casts his anchor, the anchor of his hope; and there he sticks. There the soul is kept from being hurried up and down, and carried away to split upon the rock of such a temptation. His hope holds him fast, and keeps him safe till the tempests or storms have passed over. We do not know what tempests and storms the Lord has yet reserved us unto, such, as if there is not this true hope in the text as an anchor to cast, we are likely to be split upon some rock or other. Time may come ere long that the former grace that has been opened to you as being so precious will appear precious indeed, and so this grace of hope will appear to be of some use.

In the hearts of most people, hope lies as a dead thing that is of no use at all; but if times should prove to be yet more perilous, as they may be, then it will appear of use. How many thousands of people are split upon the rocks and sands of the world merely for want of this true hope. Therefore, when they come to suffer anything in the cause of Christ, they are blown by the temptation to shift in such a sinful way. They have no anchor at all to hold them, but the temptation drives them this way and that way according as they please. When you have your anchor, and it is cast, your ship will toss up and down, but the wind cannot carry it to the sands and rocks. A Christian's heart in times of trouble and persecution may stir up and down, and may have some troubles, fears, and doubts in it; but there is something within: There is this hope as an anchor that holds the heart so that it shall not be driven upon the rocks, nor upon the sands.

Hope is like an anchor, and if ever you saw use of an anchor in your lives, then know there is a great use of this grace of hope. You may be convinced that the hopes that most men in the world have (and it may be yourselves) are but an idle dream. Have I known what it was to make use of hope as an anchor to my soul? It's impossible but some time or other you must meet with tempests and storms, strength of temptations. Now if you are acquainted with any temptations in your own hearts, you know what the use of hope as an anchor is. It would be happy for Christians, as soon as ever the temptation comes, to cast anchor presently, not to be struggling and striving to resist temptations by their own strength, but to cast anchor. So that hope is a good, a future good, and has some kind of difficulty in it. It is that which keeps the soul from sinking as the cork in the net. The lead is what sinks the net down; but the cork is what keeps the net up. So in the hearts of Christians there are many distempers, and they keep their hearts down; yet they have hope, and that keeps their hearts up. There is the efficient cause of it and the object of it.

Chapter 5

The Act of Hope

The act of hope is demonstrated in two things: quiet waiting and long expecting.

The quiet waiting of the soul: Though things seem to go cross and are long delayed, yet hope quietly waits till the storm is over and does not murmur and repine against God. It does not go out to any shifting ways, but is quiet, notwithstanding that things seem to go never so cross. Thus you have it in Psalm 40:1: "I waited patiently for the Lord; and He inclined unto me, and heard my cry." Mark what a condition the psalmist was in when he professed to waiting patiently on the Lord. Verse 2: "He brought me up also out of an horrible pit, out of the miry clay." And yet he waited patiently. Verse 5: "Many, O Lord my God, are Thy wonderful works which Thou hast done, and Thy thoughts which are to usward; they cannot be reckoned up in order unto Thee. If I would declare and speak of them, they are more than can be numbered." Then he goes on to speak of great and wonderful things that the Lord had done for him; yet see what a condition he was in. Verse 12: "For innumerable evils have compassed me about: mine iniquities have taken hold upon me, so that I am not able to look up; they are more than the hairs of my head; therefore my heart faileth me." It is as if he had said, "My heart was even ready to fail [as I said of the ship], though it is at anchor. One who has not been at sea before, when the ship is raised up by the waves and plunged down again, would think that it would even sink. And so the psalmist says, "Mine iniquities have taken hold upon me, so that I am not able to look up; they are more than the hairs of my head; therefore mine heart faileth me." And in verse 14, he speaks against the many enemies that he had at that time who would seek to destroy him, and so he prays against them. And in verse 17: "I am poor and needy; yet the Lord thinketh upon me. Thou art my help and my deliverer; make no tarrying, O my God." Yet in such a condition as he was in, he waited patiently upon the Lord.

Hope is that which quiets the heart when things seem to go quite cross and contrary, and it is called patience. Patience is the immediate fruit of hope. 1 Thessalonians 1:3 speaks of the patience of hope. That is the work of hope, to be quiet and patient under the hand of God when any evil befall us that seems to cross the things that we hope for. Hence Hebrews 10:36 says, "For ye have need of patience, that after ye have done the will of God, ye might receive the promise." Between doing the will of God and seeing the fulfilling of the promise; between making the promise and seeing it fulfilled, many things happen that cross you. You need this grace to quiet your hearts in hoping for the salvation of God when things are thus cross.

Second, there is not only a quieting of the heart, but a going out of the heart by expectation. That is, the heart goes out to look for the coming of the promise that the Lord has made. There is a metaphor in Scripture to express this second act of hope. In Philippians 1:20, the apostle speaks of hope: "According to my earnest expectation and my hope." The Greek word signifies "the stretching out of the neck," and the same word is used of the creature who expects the fullness of the redemption of the children of God in Romans 8:19. The stretching out of the creature is a similitude that is taken from a man who expects a friend to come to him, which will be of great use to him. He stands at his door and puts out his neck, looking at such a place to see whether he is coming or not. A malefactor who is ready to die, and expects a pardon to come, puts out his neck to see his friend when he comes to bring his pardon.

Expectation is putting out the neck to see when the thing will come. So the saints of God, since they have hopes of glorious things to come, so they, as it were, put out their necks to look for those glorious things that God has revealed in the Word. Hope is when the soul can quietly wait, and look after those things as the only things that he accounts his happiness to consist in. A mariner's wife dwells by the sea when the time comes that her husband should come home, and will go near the seashore and look out, because his return is a thing that she would fain have, and her mind is upon it, and so she looks out for it. So, the truth is, the hopes in the hearts of the saints above all things are upon the fulfilling of the promises of the gospel; and therefore they look for those things; their thoughts are upon them and their hearts are open for them: "Oh, when will the Lord come, and when will He fulfill such a promise?" That's the propriety of the grace of hope.

Chapter 6

The Ground of Hope

The ground of hope is the grace of faith. By faith, the soul believes a thing is so. Faith makes it to be real and true to the soul. And faith gives an interest in the thing. Those are the two acts of faith.

First, faith makes something real to the soul, convincing the soul that it is not a fancy, but a real truth. Second, faith gives an interest in that thing. It is that which belongs to me, and then hope builds upon faith. So you have it in Hebrews 11: It is the evidence of things not seen, and the substance of things hoped for. So faith gives a substantial being to what is hoped for, and hope has no bottom at all to rest upon but what faith gives.

You hope that all shall be well with you when you die, but what is the foundation of your hope? How is your hope raised? Is your hope upon the sand or upon a sure foundation? Certainly, if your hopes are true, they have a solid bottom and foundation upon which they are laid.

You will say, "What is that?"

It must be that which is made by faith in this manner. The Lord reveals to the soul the wretched condition that it is in by sin, the woeful misery that it has brought upon itself, and the breach between God and the soul. Then the Lord shows the infinite riches of His free grace in Jesus Christ unto the soul, and by His almighty power enables the soul to close with that free and rich grace of His, and then to apply it as its portion so as to rest and venture its eternal state upon that free grace of His offered. This is the work of faith.

Now once this comes into the soul, it enlightens it to see the glorious things of the covenant of grace. They are the most real things in the world, and they are made over to the soul by this grace of faith. They are such things in which my soul has an interest, such things as I can venture my soul and eternal state upon. Faith gives this foundation, and, upon this, hope is raised.

"Well, then," says the soul, "notwithstanding I have been such a wretched, vile creature as I have been, yet the Lord manifests such a blessed covenant, and such glorious free grace in His Word to receive such a guilty vile creature as I am. Oh, what a mercy is this! I am convinced of the freeness of this grace, and I have felt the Lord drawing my heart to close with it. I have found through God's mercy some ability to venture my soul and eternal state upon that free and rich grace of His offered in the covenant."

Yet the devil says, "What have you got? You have rested upon the free grace of God in Christ, but what have you gotten ever since? To sense and reason you are in as miserable a condition as you ever were!"

But then the soul says, "Aye, but this bottom I will rest upon, and upon this will I raise my hopes. I am resolved to wait upon God to my dying day, to quiet my heart in the promises that God had made unto me, and to look after the fulfilling of them. It will come, though it tarries long. I'll wait, and I'll look out for the fulfilling of them, and I am resolved to continue as long as I remain in the body."

Thus you see that hope is raised upon a foundation that faith lays. People hope that when they are sick God will deliver them, whereas indeed that is not the object of hope. Rather, a supernatural good is the proper object of hope, that which is the object of eternal life. What has given a foundation to your hope? Have you found the mighty grace of faith, the work of God's Spirit upon your souls working that precious faith? Then your hope may have something to ground itself upon. But if not, your hope is like an anchor thrown into the water that has no solid substance to rest upon. So here you have seen something about this grace of hope that we speak so much of.

The efficient cause of it is the power of the Holy Spirit. The object of it is the good of the covenant of grace, eternal Life, and that with some difficulty. And the act is quietly waiting, and the soul's expectation. Last, the ground of hope is faith, making the promises real and giving us interest in those promises. Faith is the foundation of this hope.

Hope is but the daughter of faith. If hope does not have faith as its mother, it is not of the right breed and never will do good to the soul.

The saints are men of hope. You see what their hope is, and in the opening of it you see something of the preciousness of this grace and its usefulness. They are men of hopes, and there are many considerations to manifest this by.

Chapter 7

The Saints Are Men of Hope

The saints are men of hope because:
God has excellent things to communicate, and the saints are those God has set apart to manifest Himself unto.
God has promised glorious things to the saints.
The saints are born to great hopes.
The saints are called to glorious hopes.

Certainly, the eternal God who is the Fountain of all good, who is the infinite treasure of all excellency, has infinite excellency in Himself, and delights to communicate those glorious things that are in Himself to His creatures. The creatures that God has to communicate His choice excellencies to are either angels or the children of men. Now then, if God has such things to communicate, and the children of men are the only creatures in this world that God has to let Himself out to, surely then those who are His own children by adoption must be the objects that God has set apart for the manifesting of Himself unto. Therefore they must be men of hopes, because God has so much to communicate, and there are no other creatures on earth that are capable of those glorious things but the saints. Therefore there are glorious things for them; however they appear for the present, God has great thoughts concerning them, and wishes to communicate much good to them.
Yea, not only from the nature of God, because He

has excellent things to communicate we may raise our hopes, but God has revealed glorious things that He intends to communicate to the children of men. He has promised glorious things. He has bound Himself in a way of covenant to make good most glorious things that He has promised in His Word. Yea, the saints of God have the first fruits of those glorious things already, and that's the reason for their hope. Romans 8:23: "And not only they, but ourselves also, which have the first fruits of the spirit." We have the first fruits of the Spirit; therefore we groan within ourselves, we wait for the adoption, and are saved by hope, says the text. Surely they who have received so much of the first fruits of the Spirit are men of hope.

They are men who are begotten, born to hope, and therefore are men of great hope because they are of a great birth. We used to say of such and such men who are great heirs, "Oh, such a one is born to great hopes—and those are not dead and vain hopes that are likely to come to nothing, but lively hopes." 1 Peter 1:3 is very remarkable, where the apostle speaks of the happy condition of the saints: "Blessed be the God and Father of our Lord Jesus Christ, which, according to His abundant mercy, hath begotten us again unto a lively hope by the resurrection of Jesus Christ from the dead." Mark it, "He has begotten us again into a lively hope by the resurrection of Jesus Christ from the dead." The saints not only have good things promised, but they are born to them; and a man accounts that his hopes are sure enough if he is born to great things.

All the people of God are so, you who are believers. It may be that your parents left you little or nothing in the world, but know that if you are godly you were born to great hopes, to be heirs of a kingdom, a kingdom of glory. You were born to greater things than if you were born to be the kings and queens of the whole world.

You are begotten to a lively hope. Those hopes that you have in you are not weak things nor fancies, but such as have a great deal of life in them, and should put life into your souls in the midst of all your sorrows. Yea, you are begotten to a lively hope. How? By the resurrection of Jesus Christ from the dead. You may see what the Spirit of God lays upon the hopes of the saints. If your souls have hope of life and salvation that are true hopes, that are the hopes of the saints, how did you come by them? You came by your hopes through the resurrection of Jesus Christ from the dead.

QUESTION. "How does the resurrection of Jesus Christ from the dead come to be a means of getting hopes?"

ANSWER. The resurrection of Jesus Christ from the dead is the cause of true lively hope in the hearts of the saints. By the resurrection of Jesus Christ from the dead, God has declared that He is fully satisfied for the sins of man, and that the work of redemption is fully wrought out; otherwise Christ must have been held in the prison of the grave forever. But when Jesus Christ is let out of the prison of the grave, and the bonds of death are taken from Him, this declares to men and angels that the work of redemption is perfect; it holds this out to the soul upon which faith is grounded and hope is raised. So there is an efficacy in this to work hope in the soul.

"Then," says the poor, wretched sinner, who apprehended such an infinite gulf between God and it, and saw itself through the guilt of sin sunk down into such a bottomless gulf or misery, "if God the Father shall rectify to all the world by the resurrection of Jesus Christ from the dead that He is satisfied, and that all the work is finished, why may not such a sinful wretch as I am have hope of salvation and eternal life through Him?"

Indeed the consideration of this helps the soul against that temptation of presumption, for the devil will come when a sinner begins to hope: "I hope for all this that even this vile body of mine may come to be hereafter like the body of Jesus Christ, glorious, and that I shall enjoy eternal communion with Father, Son, and Holy Spirit." It is then that the devil comes and says, "What a presumptuous wretch you are! Dare you presume that you should see the face of God at the great day with comfort, that you should be raised up to have everlasting communion with God, Christ, and the saints? What high presumption this is!"

"No," says the sinner, "I am content to own what you can charge me with in vileness and baseness. I am as vile and wretched as you can make me, but it is not presumption for me to hope because that which I make the ground and bottom of my hope is not in myself, but in the doctrine of the resurrection of our Lord Jesus Christ from the dead. The Lord Jesus Christ has come and taken my nature upon Himself, and being in the form of a servant has had the sins of the people of God laid to His charge. He has stood before the Father clad with their sins, He has satisfied the justice of God the Father and has wrought a perfect work of reconciliation and redemption. The Father has discharged Him, and He is raised now to the Heavens and sits at the right hand of God the Father, there making intercession for sinners—upon this I ground my hope. I am begotten to a lively hope through what Jesus Christ has done, and therefore, though I am never so poor, vile, and sinful, yet I have enough to raise a lively hope that I shall one day attain to such things as are written in the Book of God. Indeed the things that are written there appear to me sometimes as if they were too good to be true! How is it possible that such a wretch as I should ever attain to such great and glorious things? Were they not so great and glorious, I could hope for them."

But if you understand aright the doctrine of grace, and this resurrection of Jesus Christ from the dead, it is not the greatness of the thing that in any way should discourage your hopes, for you have enough to raise your hopes for the enjoyment of the greatest things that God is able to communicate or your soul to receive. You have encouragement to hope for these. Let the distance between them and you be never so great, yet Jesus Christ is between the Father and you, and He makes up all the distance. Therefore, by the resurrection of Christ from the dead, we are begotten to a lively hope. They are men of hope then certainly who are born to hope, and that through the resurrection of Jesus Christ from the dead.

They are called to hopes. In Ephesians 1:18, the apostle prays very earnestly that the Ephesians might understand this: "Oh, that the eyes of your understanding may be opened, that ye may know what is the hope of His calling." You are people who are called to glorious hopes, but you understand them but little. "Oh," says the apostle, "that the eyes of your understanding might be but opened, to know what is the hope of His calling, and what are the riches of the glory of His inheritance in the saints." Oh, this would be a good prayer to pray for many poor, distressed souls! Oh, they would live as men and women above the world if the eyes of their understanding were opened so that they might know what is the hope of His calling, and what riches of the glory of His inheritance in the saints are.

And besides that, there is a further evidence that the saints are certainly men of hopes, because they so constantly follow after God in the midst of all discouragements that they can endure so much persecution and rejoice so much in tribulations, and nothing can take their hearts away from God. If they did not have hopes, certainly it would be impossible that they could go on following after God, that they could endure so much persecution here in this world. It is an evidence that they are men of hopes because they receive so little from God in this world. You know the apostle's argument: "If we had hope only in this world, we were the most miserable of all men."

Do you not see how the saints of God are persecuted and condemned? The thing that the devil would labor to beat down our hopes with is the very thing that the apostle labors to help to raise our hopes upon. The devil says, "If you are sons and daughters of God, why does God let the devil and ungodly men prevail over you?"

The saints should turn the reasoning back upon the devil in this manner: "Does God allow the devil and wicked men to prevail upon us now? Surely then God has reserved great things for us hereafter."

The devil says, "Surely God does not regard you; and it is but a fancy for you to hope, seeing that God leaves you so here."

"Nay," says the believer, "because God suffers me to be afflicted so here, therefore there are glorious things coming. If we had hope in this life only, of all men we would be most miserable."

I might give various other evidences to prove that the saints are men of hope, but for now let me give a word or two of application.

Chapter 8

The Use of the First Doctrine

Bless God for those hopes that He gives you in this world. The Lord might have intended glorious things hereafter and never revealed them to you here; but blessed be God that He gives us this hope to keep us from sinking, as He gave the sun to rule the day and the moon to rule the night. I remember a learned man allegorized thus upon it: "God gives us the moon of hope to guide us in the night of affliction." We know that moonlight is never uncomfortable. The Sun of righteousness is to arise ere long in the morning of our resurrection, but in this life we have our hope to guide us in our night of affliction. Oh, blessed be God for revealing this unto us, and for giving us such a good ground and bottom of our hope that we may hope for such great things without fear of presumption.

Let all the saints of God be looked upon as happy creatures. You see them as mean in the world and poor. Aye, but know that they are men of hope. You look upon princes with honorable respect, and look so upon every child of God as one who has a precious soul, who has great hopes to come hereafter. You hope in men, but they fail; and you hope in the creatures, and they fail; yet here's the hope of the saints: they have an Anchor that shall never fail. You are afraid, perhaps, of stronger temptations that you have heard others have suffered shipwreck upon. And a poor sinner asks, "What shall I do when temptations and persecutions come, when ill times come, and all the props of the creature are taken away?" The reason why so many split upon the rocks this way and that is either because they have no Anchor, or else it was of brittle metal. But if you have this hope, never fear; for it will hold your soul from suffering shipwreck in the greatest storms and tempests.

Alexander would give away all that he had for the present. And some asked him what he would keep for himself. "I have hope for myself," said he. And so indeed it should cause the people of God to rejoice in their hope, and be content with anything that they have. You have enough to make you rich, so manifest it by living above the world in your conduct, by not being overly troubled for the loss of the creature, or anything else. Oh, manifest hereby that you are a man or woman who is born to great hopes. Hebrews says that Christians have a city, that is, another city besides this one here: "For they that say such things declare plainly that they seek a country, and truly if they had been mindful of the country that they came out of, they might have had opportunity to have returned, but they plainly declare in living so above the world as pilgrims and strangers here, that they seek another country."

And so, my brethren, Christians should plainly declare to all the world that they seek another country, that their hopes are not here. Do you live so? I appeal to your consciences, are your lives such as plainly declare before all the world that there's another country that you seek? We see that most Christians care for the world, and so pine at the loss of any creature comfort, as if they had no other hopes in this life. But now it becomes Christians to use the world as if they used it not, with indifference of spirit, because of the great hopes that they have, and they account their riches to be in another country. Woe to a soul if a man has no other hopes than he has in this world.

We should never be troubled if God takes away this and the other comfort; yet God requires us to spend freely of what we have because we have hopes of resurrection. The truth is, this is one special reason why God does not so much care to have His people prosper in the world. God says, "I have laid up that for them that will pay for all at last."

As regards the wicked, God does not care if they have their heart's desire. He says, "I have an eternity hereafter to torment them; let them prosper here for a while if they will."

On the other hand, what if the saints suffer? God says, "I have an eternity of happiness for them hereafter, and I know when they come to possess all their hopes they will never think that I was a hard Master. I have enough to pay for all their sorrows and troubles that they meet with in My ways."

Chapter 9

The Second Doctrine

DOCTRINE. Every man who has this hope purifies himself. The word is not "sanctifies himself," but "purifies himself." Christ is said to sanctify Himself, who has no sin; but purifying implies a want of holiness, and that there is uncleanness and filthiness.

In this second point, there are four particulars:

First, sin is a pollution and a defilement.

Second, the best saints in this world, who have the best hopes, have remainders of sin and uncleanness.

Third, they cleanse themselves.

Fourth, the hope that they have is that which causes them to cleanse themselves.

If he who has this hope purifies himself, then sin is uncleanness; it is filthiness. In Matthew 15, says Christ Himself in verse 20, "These are the things which defile a man: that which proceeds out of the heart, the evils that flow from that unclean fountain; these are the things that defile a man." Sin is called uncleanness and filthiness in the very abstract; and it is compared in Scripture to all kinds of filthiness: to vomit, mire, menstruous clothes, sores, wounds that have filthy matter in them, and many such things.

The impurity of sin consists, first, in the contrariety that it has to the holiness of God. It is the only thing that is contrary to God's infinite holiness, and to His pure nature. Second, it is the corruption and rottenness of a man's soul. Third, sin is the mixture of the soul with that which is more base and vile than the soul, and that defiles the soul. When your clothes have dirt on them, there is something on them worse than the clothes which defiles them; but if there were gold or silver lace, that does not defile. Men do not think that gold defiles the cloth because it is better than the cloth. It is no defiling of silver if it is mixed with gold, but it is if it be mixed with lead.

The mixture of the soul with God, with heavenly things, does not defile it, but makes the soul more pure and more excellent. But the mixture of the soul with sinful ways, with lusts, and with the creature does defile it; for the soul mixes itself with that which is worse than itself. Thus the soul comes to be defiled as silver is defiled with lead, and the saints see sin as the greatest defilement of anything in the world because they see into the infinite purity of God's nature, into the purity of the law, and into the excellency of their own souls— and therefore they see sin to be filthy. It is such a filthiness as makes the creature loathsome in the eyes of God, for the creature is not loathsome in God's eyes by any bodily defilement. One that cleans gutters or who sweeps chimneys is not loathsome in God's eyes. He may be more glorious in God's eyes, if he is godly, than the prince upon his throne, if he is wicked.

Though outward defilements make us loathsome in the eyes of one another, yet not in the eyes of God. But sin is such an uncleanness that it makes us abominable in the eyes of God. If we come into His presence with the filth of our sins, He abhors us. He turns His face from us; yea, sin defiles all things we touch, like the defilement of leprosy. It is that which pollutes the whole world, and therefore the world must be purged and purified by fire; yea, it is such a defilement that nothing but the blood of Him who is the Son of God can wash it away; such a defilement that all the water in the sea cannot wash away, only the blood of Jesus Christ, who cleanses from all sin. Oh, what a defilement is here!

Application

USE 1. Hence we learn how to judge and esteem those who go on in the course of sin, who are wallowing in sin like swine wallowing in the mire. They are filthy, loathsome, and abominable creatures, however neat they may be. You may be neat and spruced, and cannot endure to have a spot upon your clothes; yet, in the meantime, you have that filthiness and nastiness that makes you loathsome in the eyes of the eternal God, yea, and in the eyes of the saints, so far as they are able to see. In Proverbs 13:5, we have such an expression: "A righteous man hateth lying, but a wicked man is loathsome, and cometh to shame." As a wicked man loves lying, it makes him loathsome; he stinks above ground. A liar especially is looked upon as a pest. You see men who, for their own ends, will lie; even that sin makes him loathsome when it comes to be discovered in the eyes of all with whom he converses. And so it is with all other wicked men: they are loathsome before the Lord.

USE 2. The consideration of this should teach us to take heed of sin, and to be watchful over our ways, especially when we live among those who are filthy and unclean. The better your garments are, the more careful you are of keeping them from filth. One that has a fine new garment is very careful to preserve it from spots, stains, and dust. You do not care if your old clothes are dirty, but new ones you are more careful of. Certainly, if your souls were renewed, if you were made new creatures, if you had the new robes of our eldest

Brother upon you, if the image of God were drawn upon you, you would be very careful to keep yourselves from spots. If you have a piece of board in your house, though there are spots of dirt upon it, you do not care; but if you have a curious picture drawn upon it, then spots of dirt you would account to be a great evil. So, where the image of God is drawn upon the soul, there spots and uncleanness are worse than anywhere else. And in that regard the sins of God's people are worse than the sins of any. The finer any cloth is, the worse it is when stained. If you have a stain upon a coarse piece of linen, you will not care. For men of the world who do not know the excellency of their souls, though they are defiled, it is not so much; but the saints who have refined souls, pure souls, through the graces of the Spirit of God, their souls are made precious. Oh, they should account sin to be a great evil to them because it is a defilement to such precious souls as they have! And therefore, as soon as ever they have committed a sin, they do not lie in it; for sin, since it is filthiness, soaks into the heart.

You know that when you have a stain, you will immediately labor to get it out. Oh let no evil of sin soak into your spirits, but as soon as you have received any spot in your souls, immediately apply the warm blood of Jesus Christ to your soul, which cleanses us from all sin (1 John 1:7). It is not "hath cleansed," or "will cleanse," but "cleanseth," present tense, daily. Neither is it simply "from sin," but "from all sin." Oh, run to this Fountain that was opened for sin, and for uncleanness. Christ's blood is not yet dry, but is of as powerful and cleansing a nature now as it was the first moment it was shed upon the cross.

Chapter 10

The Saints of God Have Remaining Sin in Them

The second thing that is implied is that there is some remainder of sin even in the hearts of the sons of God who, having true hopes wrought in them by the Holy Spirit, and ere long shall see Jesus Christ as He is, and will be made like Him, have some defilements remaining in them while they live here in this world. It may be said of every child of God as Christ said to His disciples, "You are clean, but not all; you are cleansed and sanctified, but not thoroughly." It cannot be said of any child of God here as it was said of Absalom, that from the crown of the head to the sole of the foot he had no spot in him; he was so comely, and yet, by the way, Absalom was a reprobate for all that. It cannot be said so of any while they remain in a world that lies in wickedness. The filth of sin has so soaked into the hearts of men that until there is a dissolution of body and soul, it cannot be quite purged away. God indeed justifies His saints perfectly at first, but He sanctifies them by degrees. "He that saith he hath no sin lies, and the truth of God is not in him." I need not try to prove it, experience proves it sufficiently.

USE 1. Then let all the saints of God walk humbly before God. Though God has endued you with hope and much grace, yet still look upon your black feet; you have a great deal of evil to be humbled for. God has good ends why He reserves sin in the hearts of the saints. He brings out His own glory from it.

USE 2. See cause for daily renewing your repentance

and your faith in the blood of Jesus Christ. Do not think it enough that once you believed, or once you repented. Many people think that if ever they repented of their sins, that will serve turn for all the time of their lives. Oh, if you believe that, you are not acquainted with the way of God in the hearts of the saints! These graces are to be renewed daily.

God has wrought faith in you, yet God expects that you should daily act your faith upon Jesus Christ for the cleansing of your soul to the extent that you defile your soul daily. You do not go about the least duty without contracting some filth. Your houses every day gather filth and dust at least. Though swine are not allowed to come into your houses, yet they gather some kind of uncleanness every day, and need to be swept and washed daily. So you need to wash your soul in the blood of Christ every day, and you need to renew your repentance every day.

Afterwards, in the life that is to come, you shall never renew any act of repentance or act of faith upon the blood of Christ to cleanse your soul; but this is your work now, and it would be of marvelous use if we would so look upon it as to know what is our work every day. We could not lie down in peace unless our consciences can tell us that this day we have renewed some act of faith and repentance for the cleansing of our souls. We should not let our filthiness and uncleanness go on long, but presently renew the acts of faith and repentance.

USE 3. If there remains some filth and uncleanness still in our hearts, it should teach us to long for heaven, when our sanctification shall be made as perfect as our justification is. The saints of God will not make any ill use, but a good use of this point, that there are relics of sin in them. Indeed, carnal hearts, upon hearing such a point, grow more hard, and think they have all the faith needed. The best need to be purified; they have some dross mixed with their silver. The Preacher tells us, "There's not one who has the best hopes that is without sin." Thus carnal hearts will make an ill use of it. It may be that you live in a course of sin, yet you put it off with this, that the best have their sins. Though you can vex and be troubled for the loss of a coin or sixpence, yet you are not much troubled for your sin.

To address this, I shall hint four things to you in the next chapter.

Chapter 11

Answers to Those Who Live in a Course of Sin

OBJECTION. "But the best of men have some sin."

ANSWER. Since the best of men have some sin, therefore you hope that all is well with you? The worst of all may have some good in them, just as the saints have had some ill in them. So you hope that, notwithstanding your evil, you may go to heaven. Then I tell you that some reprobates have had more good in them than you have; and notwithstanding your good you may go to hell.

OBJECTION. "Lot, Peter, and David had sin, and yet they went to heaven."

ANSWER. Aye, but Saul, Ahab, Judas, and Herod had more good in them than you have, and yet they perished. When did you do as much good as Ahab did? When the prophet threatened him in the name of God the text says he humbled himself in sackcloth and went softly. Herod heard John the Baptist gladly, and reformed many things. Oh, he loved to hear John, and he reverenced John. Have you done so? Judas was troubled for his sin, and came and made restitution of that which he had wrongfully gotten. Have you done so? Never tell me of some sin in the saints as being your comfort. Rather, look upon the good that was in the wicked and reprobate, and see whether that is not more for your discouragement.

OBJECTION. "The saints have sin remaining in them as well as I do."

ANSWER. But what if your sin should prove to be a

sin unto death? There's a great deal of difference in sin. Suppose a women should have her husband lie dead and stiff, with no breath at all. And suppose that one should come and say to her, "Why are you troubled? Many men are stiff with cold, and hold their breath a great while."

"Oh, but," she says, "he is dead. The stiffness is the stiffness of death, and his breath is quite gone." She will not be put off with the fact that some are stiff with cold, and some hold their breath. So you speak of the sins that you have, and that the saints have sin. But your sin may be the sin that proceeds from death, and not from infirmity and weakness. Deuteronomy 32:5: "They have corrupted themselves; their spot is not the spot of his children." You have spots and defilements in you that are not the spots of God's children. To show the difference between the spots of wicked men and the spots of the saints would require a large treatise; but I'll mention this now so that men may not presume and think themselves safe because the best of men have some sin. But let them check themselves with this: Is my spot the spot of God's children? It may be my sin is of another nature; my sin may prove to be the sin to death, and theirs may be but an infirmity."

OBJECTION. "Those who are godly and have true grace have some sin remaining in them."

ANSWER. I have never found in Scripture, nor do I think any example can be found of any who had such a sin in them to plead for their sin, and to harden themselves in their sin, because other saints had sin as well as they. You shall not find this in Scripture, and you shall not find this among the saints. Though they have some sin in them, yet not this sin of pleading for their sin, and hardening themselves in their sin, upon the consideration that other saints have sin as well as they. No, they rather are the more afraid and troubled for their sin. If you had an ingenious spirit in you, you would rather reason thus, "Oh, Lord, is it so that Thou art not only dishonored by the men of the world who do not know Thee, but the best of Thy people carry about with them a body of death; and shall I add to the sin that is committed in the world? Thou hast dishonor enough, and I should take to heart that Thou art dishonored by any, especially by Thy own children. And shall that which should be the matter of my grief and mourning be the hardening of me in my sins? Oh, how contrary is this to the ingenuity of a Christian!"

Yes, the saints have their sins, but how are they affected with them? Paul had his sin, but how was he affected? "Oh, wretched man that I am, who shall deliver me from this body of death?" You never find him crying out that he was a wretched man because he was hungry and naked, and suffered persecution; but his sin made him so. Is it so with you? Does your remaining sin make you seek God, and account yourself in the most wretched condition because of it? How you are perplexed and troubled for the loss of your estate, and for any evil that befalls you! But you agree well enough with your sin, and think that it is nothing but that which the saints have.

Will people be satisfied with that when they are plundered of all their estates and abused? "I am plundered no more than others are"? The truth is, we ought to comfort ourselves that indeed, though we suffer, yet we suffer not so much as others saints of God have suffered in former times. We may reason so in our sufferings, but not reason thus by our sin. We should rather account our sins the worse because God is dishonored by others as well as by us.

Chapter 12

The Saints Purge Themselves From Sin

After conversion, the saints have a principle contrary to sin; it is an active principle; and it is a powerful principle against sin.

Though the saints have sin in them, yet they purge themselves. 2 Timothy 2:21: "If a man therefore purge himself from these, he shall be a vessel unto honor, sanctified, and meet for the Master's use, and prepared unto every good work." The vessels of honor that are in God's house, God delights to make any use of. They are such as purge themselves; not only such as are made clean, but such as purge themselves. In God's house, the vessels that God takes delight in, that come to His table, must not be filthy, nasty vessels. God would not have such come to Him, but vessels that are fit for the Master's use are such as are purged; yea, they purge themselves.

OBJECTION. Can a man purify himself? Is it not God who must cleanse and sanctify us? Isaiah 1:25: I shall "purely purge away thy dross, and take away all thy tin." That is God's promise. It is fulfilled spiritually to the hearts of the saints; the Lord comes, and He purely purges away the dross, and takes away their tin from them.

ANSWER. The acts of God upon the hearts of His saints are in such a manner as though they are God's acts, yet God is pleased to have them be the actions of His people. So gracious is God to His people that those things that He helps them do He will account as their actions. Philippians 2:12–13: "Work out your own salva-

tion with fear and trembling, for it is God which wor-
keth in you both to will and to do of His good pleasure." You work, for it is God who works in you; though
God works in you, yet it is you who works too. The
saints are said to work. And this may be very profitable
and useful to us to take away that lazy kind of reasoning
that is in many people. They sit still and do nothing,
and they can do nothing without God. "What can we
do? It is God who must do all. How can we get power
over our sins? God must do it!" So upon that they sit
still and do nothing.

My text says that he purges himself. Oh, do not
stand reasoning so. God calls you to do it as if you were
to do it yourself alone. That man purifies himself; and
if you belong to God, God does put a principle into you
so that you are able to do it. Not without God, that is
true; you cannot put a bit of meat into your mouths
without God. Though it is God who does all, yet God
puts a principle into the new creature so that he is able
to stir and live suitably to the nature of a new creature.

What's the difference between a live thing and a
dead thing? A dead thing is that which has no moving
in itself at all. That's the difference between life and no
life: One has a spirit in itself to move, and the other has
none. One who has life has received a principle in itself to move. Clocks have no principle within, but the
weights that hang down move them. But watches have a
spring within to move them. So the saints have a principle in them so that they are able to purify themselves.
It is true, God first comes upon them, and they are
merely passive; at first God comes and shows to them
the evil of their sin, holds over them the wrath that is
due for their sins, and causes sin to be bitter and terrible to them. He shows it in the dreadful visage of it.
"Look, here's the sin that you take such delight and
content in. See what it brings you to." By degrees God

makes men weary of their sin.

Afterwards, the Lord comes by His almighty power, and deadens the bitter root that was in the soul, mortifies it, and so puts a principle of grace into the soul that now it is able to live for Him. At first we are merely passive, but when God has done that first work of His, then He puts a principle into us to act. We need a continual supply, but see all the assistance that the saints have from God to help them against their sin. It is not to put new principles into them, but to stir up those principles that God puts in them at their conversion. As soon as God converts any soul, He puts a principle of grace contrary to every sin in them. There is no sin that the soul is inclined to but at the very first moment of conversion there is a principle of grace put into the soul contrary to every sin. Therefore that person purifies himself on these three considerations:

First, because it is a principle contrary to sin, and one contrary will seek to get out another one. In wicked and ungodly men, sin is with them as their nature, as poison is in a toad; but though the saints have sin in them, yet it is in them as their sickness, and they have a contrary nature besides their sinful nature. They have a sinful nature, but they are partakers of the divine nature, and that opposes the sinful nature as fire does water. The saints have that principle contrary to sin as fire is to water, and it is impossible but that principle within them must be consuming their sin and so purifying them.

Second, as it is contrary to sin, so it is an active principle or grace; for it is the divine nature, and the divine nature is a pure act. God is a pure act, and the divine nature that we have partakes much of God. It is very much like God, and therefore must be very active and stirring. If water runs, though filth comes into it, yet it is quickly clear again because it is running. If all the filth that runs into the Thames River should stay there, and the water in the Thames should stand still for just two or three days, it would be ready to poison us all. But because it is running, it is in some measure cleansed, and it is not so noisome as otherwise it would be.

When the wicked and ungodly have sin in them, it comes into them as filthy water, and there it putrefies. But the saint's sin is as a running water, the principle that they have is stirring in them, and so comes to be cleansing. Indeed, the more active Christians are, the more clean. Christians, if you would be clean, let grace be active. If grace is stirring and active, you will be clean. A man who is most active and stirring usually has the most clean body, and people who stir but little find diseases growing on them. Grace makes the saints active and stirring, and so by that means they purify themselves.

Third, the principle is a powerful principle; it is contrary and active, and very strong in them, for it is the divine nature, and that must be very powerful. If a man has poison in his body, yet, if he has a strong heart, he may work out his poison. Some who have a sickness yet, having strong natures, work out the venom that was within them. So the saints, though they are weak (in comparison with others) and have not so much strength as others saints have, yet there is not the weakest saint but has the divine nature in them, and therefore has that in them that is stronger than corruptions and will work out corruptions in time. It is the divine nature, therefore surely the children of God purify themselves; for first it is contrary to sin, and so active and strong. Then, having the assistance of God with them, and the strength of the covenant of grace to go along with them, so they must be able to purify themselves.

Chapter 13

What the Saints Do When They Purify Themselves

QUESTION. What is the work of a gracious heart when it is purifying itself?

ANSWER 1. First, such a heart is truly willing, yea, and takes pain to know the worst of itself, and to find out all the secret corners where any filth of heart may possibly lie. That's the first work of a saint when he goes about to purify himself. He does not lie down sullenly and heavily, and say, "Lord I can do nothing; it must be Thy work to sanctify me." No, but he stirs up and is doing, and falls about the work. He finds that he has an abundance of sin and uncleanness. The first thing that he does is to search: "Oh, that I could find out where all the poison of sin lies; there are many windings and turnings in my heart, and a great deal of filth lies there."

In a man's garments, not only filth and dirt gets in, but if you should rip the garment and look into every seam and fold, there you would see the dust gathered. So it is in the heart: one who has a gracious heart will purify himself. He not only takes notice of sins that are in plain view, that every one can see as well as himself, but he will get into his own heart and search and examine every faculty of soul. "What sin is there in my mind? Are not some mistakes in my mind the cause of some evil that is in my heart and life? What sin is there in my conscience and in my thoughts?"

With the abundance of evil that is there, he will quickly find a sink of sin in the life. Sinful affections are carried upon wrong objects, and taken off from the right object. They are fickle and inconstant in that way. There is sin in the members of the body, the very eyes, ears, hands, and feet. The gracious soul will search and try what filth it can find in every secret corner; it takes pains, and makes its work to find out all. He is not troubled if anybody will come and tell him that they are afraid that if he will examine his heart in such and such a thing, that he shall find a great deal of filth that he did not know of before. One who is gracious will be glad that he may be in any way helped to find any filthiness that he did not see in himself before. Would anybody be offended if one should come and tell him that there was a spot on his face? He would thank you if you would tell him that; so a gracious heart would thank any who shall help him find out his corruptions.

ANSWER 2. What a gracious heart does in purifying itself is to join and side with every truth of God by which it comes to be sanctified. Every truth, though it is never so hard a truth, and seems to be never so terrible, yet a gracious soul blesses God for it and is glad in it. He is glad it is a truth, and that it pleases God to reveal such a truth unto him. "Before I knew this, there was a great deal of evil that lay in my heart, and it was likely to lie longer. But I hope this truth will help me against many corruptions in my heart that I did not understand before."

And in his siding with every truth, he is not only glad for it, but will seek to maintain every truth of God that works against his corruptions. Many men and women, when they come to some conviction of some truth that works against some of their corruptions, if they should come into any company and hear any body object against it, they are secretly glad that they have an objection against it. But when a gracious heart has gotten a truth that tends to purge out corruptions, it will maintain the truth against objections.

It will apply that truth; it will not keep it only in the understanding, soaring aloft, but apply it and lay it home to the heart. "Oh, my soul, take notice of this truth; it concerns you nearly!" And so lays it upon the sore wherein it knows itself to be most guilty.

It submits to the truth. "It is the truth of God, and though it will pluck away such a corruption wherein I have had so much content, yet it is the truth of God, and I will submit to it."

It will continue and hold the truth upon the heart when the heart would be weary of that truth. Sometimes you will find that, if you observe your own hearts in applying some truths, your hearts, through their corruption, will be weary of some searching truth and will be ready to cast it off. But a gracious heart holds it up, and will have the truth continue upon his heart, for the corruption is not eaten out. A child who has a plaster upon a sore, if it smarts a little, will be ready to pluck it off; but let it stay on till it is well, and then it will fall off on its own accord. So a heart that desires to purify itself keeps on the truths of God. Though they are painful, yet it keeps them on to draw away the corruption that is in the soul. That's the second work of one who purifies himself: it sides with every truth of God that works against his corruptions.

ANSWER 3. A gracious heart uses all the ability it has to oppose sin in the soul and will let none lie idle. If God has given unto it any parts of nature, memory, natural understanding, or natural judgment, it stirs up all of them. If there are any common gifts of God's Spirit, it stirs them all to get out the sin that is in the soul. It does not hold it a light matter, as most people do. "We are all sinners. God be merciful to us. I wish we could do better," and such kind of words, and so makes sin a light thing. But what do you do to get out your sin? Do you stir up all that is within you, all your parts, common gifts, and graces, and set them all to work so that you may purge and cleanse your heart from sin? And all is little enough, for sin so twists itself into the hearts of the children of men and leavens them that it's all little enough to get out the corruptions from the soul. Indeed, there's no such need of such a stir to keep the soul from the acts of gross sins in the world; that may be done without such ado. But if you will come to purify yourself as Christ is pure, there must be all this ado. And a gracious heart finds need of all this; and that heart that does not find the need of this has cause to suspect that it does not understand the way of God in the hearts of the saints.

ANSWER 4. The heart that purifies itself takes up every duty that God requires, delights in all means and helps that God affords him, and makes use of them all to cleanse it from its sin. Do not think that because Christ must work all, therefore what need do we have to perform any duties. Do not account them as duty-mongers who make conscience of duties. But those who slight them so have not found the benefit of them for themselves, and therefore they think that others should not make such conscience of them, as appears in their loose carriage. Observe the ways and the lives of those who slight duties so much, and how quickly unclean they grow. There is not that graciousness in their conduct as formerly. But the saints find that in duty performed in a holy way they draw nigh to God and have communion with Him, and so find that God conveys Himself through duties of cleansing the heart.

Duties are the pipes and conduits through which God is pleased to convey Himself; and they provide grace and power for cleansing the heart. God conveys His water through these pipes for cleansing the heart, and therefore a gracious heart will set upon every duty.

If it has tried one and cannot find power by that, it falls to another, and every ordinance, and ordinary and extraordinary duties. There are some things that are so foul that ordinary things will not cleanse them. You wash and scour them, but all the water in the world will not make them clean. So there is a cleansing of the heart by ordinary duties, and by extraordinary duties. Make this the aim and end of your heart in using means to cleanse sin: "Why do I come to the Word? Oh, that the Word might meet with my sin, and that God would bless the Word to convey something to my soul to cleanse it, to purify my heart. It comes to the Word for the very end that it might get sin cleansed; when it comes to the sacrament, it is for that very end. Oh, I have such and such corruptions that prevail against me, and I cannot get power over them, so now I come to this other ordinance to see what the blood of Jesus Christ will do to cleanse my soul." Before it comes to such an ordinance, the soul propounds this end to itself.

I appeal to your consciences: when you go to prayer, can you say that this is one great end that you go to prayer? "Oh, that by this ordinance of God I might get some power over such corruption, over my passions, over my deadness of heart! When I go to the Word, I go for this very end." As you propound this to yourselves, so if you indeed follow this work of purifying your hearts as you ought, when you are at the duty, you observe there the way of God towards you, whether God comes in to you, according to what you do desire; whether you feel God taking your hearts away from your sin and letting in something of His Spirit into your souls to strengthen you against it. Then, after you are done, you look back to see what you have gotten. Suppose you pray against passion. What have you gotten by it? Are you more humbled? Then you should be troubled in your heart because God absents Himself from you, and does not grant unto you that which you aim at.

ANSWER 5. A gracious heart is willing to endure any difficulty to gain any power against his sin. He is willing to suffer anything. "If the performance of holy duties will not do it, and if ordinances will not do it; if the Lord is pleased to lay His hand of afflictions upon me, let Him bring a fiery trial if that may purge me." Isaiah 27:9 says that the fruit of afflictions is to purge away the sin of the church. Oh, once a gracious heart finds this, how willing such a one is to be afflicted! Yea, the main thing that quiets the hearts of the saints in their afflictions is this: "Oh, I hope that the Lord intends nothing other than to purge away my sin, and if this is God's intention, let Him do with me what He will. Fire purges away dross from metal when other things cannot do it; and God sees that I have a vile wretched heart, and I must have afflictions to purge away my sin: The will of the Lord be done, and I account all my losses made up if the loss of the dearest thing I have in the world may but help me with power against such a corruption."

Indeed, this is the way that the saints have to make up what they have lost in the creature. When God plucks away a child, or anything that is dear, a carnal heart thinks it is impossible to have such a loss made up. "Oh, but if God will just sanctify this affliction to take away my sin, I shall account it as great a good as I had before. So what if I suffer pain, am troubled, and have greater afflictions than others? If God by this takes away my sin, I am willing to suffer anything."

You who have some stains in your linen clothes are willing on frosty nights to lay them outside, and that makes them look white. So it may be with your souls: you have so defiled your souls with sin that it is not a little dirt that may be soon wiped away that is upon you; but the filth of sin has stained your hearts, and the Lord lays you out to frost so that He might cleanse you. So when you are willing to endure anything in the world to be cleansed, this is purifying yourselves. And then not only afflictions from God's hands, but from men's hands too. If God should use wicked men to afflict you never so much, they are God's wisps to scour His people withal, and so to take away their sin. Still they are base and vile, and as soon as God has done with them He will throw the wisp upon the dunghill.

ANSWER 6. A gracious heart labors against all sins, but especially against his chief and master sin, the sin of his complexion and constitution, against that which he finds the most his corrupt nature most inclined to— he labors to cleanse himself from that one more than any. Many people will labor to cleanse themselves from gross sins that they are disgraced by, that everybody takes notice of to their dishonor; but there is one special bosom sin that they think they could not part withal. Now one who has this hope, who sees one sin more than another suitable to nature, lays the chief strength that he has against that sin, against this darling sin, knowing that if he can but purge out that, the other noisome humors will follow. Many go to work like unskillful physicians: They purge out the humor that is the effect of the disease, but they do not purge out the humor that is the cause of the disease. So unskillful Christians look at sins that are the effect of such a corruption, but they never look at the sin that is the cause of that corruption.

ANSWER 7. A gracious heart purifies itself not only by doing this, but it must endeavor to act its faith upon the blood of Jesus Christ, and look upon the application of the blood of Jesus Christ to its soul as that which puts an efficacy and life to all the other.

You may ask, "Can a man apply the blood of Jesus Christ to his soul before he has purified himself? Must he first purify himself, and then apply it?"

No, a man may lawfully, without any presumption, apply the blood of Jesus Christ to his soul though he is never so vile, if he applies it to take away the filth of sin as well as the guilt of sin. This a true Christian does not only because the blood of Christ will make peace between God and him, and that the blood of Christ has in it a virtue to cleanse from sin, but because it is the blood of Christ that gives an efficacy to all other means and all other ordinances. So he goes about to purify himself. What's the reason that many of you who have sought to cleanse yourselves have been troubled for your sins? You have been upon your sickbeds, and there you have cried out bitterly for your sins; there you have resolved against them, and you have spoken from your hearts then, yet nothing has come upon it. But you rest in your own endeavors, and do not look upon the blood of Christ as that which gives efficacy to all your endeavors and resolutions. You must do that. He who has this hope purifies himself.

Such a soul is restless and will never be quiet till something is done. He has made use of these means. "Well, I have done this a long time," says one, "and I find nothing comes of it." But he will never listen to such a temptation, but goes on continually working, and resolves he will not neglect anything. "Oh, I shall carry the striving of my heart against my corruption to my grave" is the resolution of a gracious heart. Though the body is weary and the flesh, yet it goes on pursuing its enemy, and nothing can give rest to it. It's not what we have in the world, or what comforts we have in our families; nothing can give rest to the heart but the cleansing it from sin. "I have been abroad in company and defiled myself by such a sin, and have made myself the more unfit for communion with God. Therefore, nothing that I have can content my soul till I have gotten it in some measure cleansed." Now when the ground of your ease and quiet is from your purging yourself from sin, that's ease and quiet indeed.

You will say, "I have labored and gotten nothing."

Do not wrong the grace of God; let these things be done, and the soul will certainly get way against sin. It may be not just in that particular, but in something or other, either one grace or other active and stirring. A physician may cleanse the body of a great many filthy humors, and yet the patient not feel it presently; in fact, he may feel his body in a worse condition than he was before he was meddled with. He may then come to the physician and say, "Oh, sir, that which you gave me has done me more harm than good."

"Why? How did it work?" says he.

"It wrought thus and thus," you say.

"Oh, do not trouble yourself, for do you think that I can do away with all these ill humors at once? Before, all the ill humors lay still, and so they did not pain you, and were more dangerous then. But now some come to be taken away, and all the others are stirred. That's the reason you find yourselves worse than you were before."

So it is with the soul that is thus seeking to purify itself. Perhaps while laboring, such a one says, "I never found myself worse in all my life, never more wandering, more deadness, more corruptions stirring." But the truth is, this is but the stirrings of the humor, and there is a great deal of hope that something has been purged away; for the text says that he who has this hope desires not only to purify himself, and wishes and prays that he might purify himself, but he does purify himself. There is an actual purifying, for certainly God will not be wanting to a heart that goes upon this work in this way. And thus you have the working of the heart in purifying itself.

The main thing that hardens others in their sin is their hope: They hope that they shall be saved when they die and that God loves them; therefore they are secure in their evil and sinful way. The hope of the wicked is the very thing that makes them more secure in their evil ways.

The hope of God's mercies that the saints have is the thing whereby they come to purge out corruption; yea, to purify themselves as Jesus Christ is pure.

Chapter 14

The Saints' Hope Makes Them Purify Themselves

The hope of the saints makes them purify themselves. The hope of the saints is of such high, great, wonderful, and glorious things. Their hopes are great, and therefore elevate their hearts. Their hopes being great and high makes them jealous of anything that may contradict their hopes. The greatness of their hope fills their hearts with comfort, and therefore it purifies. The greatness of their hope purges their hearts because it inflames their spirits with love to God.

There are a great many reasons why those who are the people of God should endeavor to purge all sin out of their hearts, and not to live in any known sin, but make it their work to set themselves against every sinful way. But the thing that I am now to show is how the hope that they have of seeing the face of God, and enjoying so much mercy from God another day is that which cleanses their hearts. We have divers Scriptures to show that this is that which cleanses the hearts of the saints. In Psalm 37:3, the Scripture joins these two actions together as having a special relation one unto another: "Trust in the Lord, and do good." Doing good is the fruit of trusting or hoping in the Lord, for hope is the daughter of faith. Psalm 78:7: "That they might set their hope in God, and not forget the works of God, but keep His commandments." Note what follows "that they might set their hope in God"—"and not forget His works, but keep His commandments." The soul that sets his hope on God will not forget His works, but will endeavor to keep His commandments. So in 1 Peter 3:15–16, likewise you have these two together: "But sanctify the Lord God in your hearts, and be ready always to give an answer to every man that asketh you a reason of the hope that is in you with meekness and fear, having a good conscience." Those who are able to give a reason for the hope that is in them are such as have a good conscience; a good conscience and a grounded hope are always joined together. That man or woman who does not have a good conscience is not able to give a reason for the hope that is in them. You hope that God will have mercy upon you, and that all will be well at last; but can you give a reason for your hope? Certainly upon that, all depends; for if your hopes should fail, you are lost forever. Are you able to give a reason for it? Will you lay the weight of your eternal estate upon that for which you are not able to give a good reason?

Every man and woman, when they think of the hope of God's mercies, should ask, "What reason am I able to give for it?" Certainly your hopes must be examined one day before the Lord, and His blessed angels and saints. They must be examined, and therefore it is good for you now to think what reason you are able to give of it. If there is not a good conscience, there can be no reason given for it. We might name many reasons why these two are joined together, hope and godliness; but the main work is to show you what there is in this hope that works the heart unto holiness, and that causes the heart to purify itself, even as Christ is pure.

"He that hath this hope purifies himself, even as Christ is pure." It is so great a hope since, wheresoever it is truly, it is a hope of such great and high things. The wonderful and glorious things that are the objects of this hope cannot but purge the heart from the filth of sin. Oh, the difference that there is in the state of the soul before this hope came into it, and when this hope is in it! "Before I was a vile wretched worm, one who was a child of wrath and under the curse of the Law, one liable to all the fruits of God's eternal wrath, to be a castaway forever for all I knew. And the Lord now has given me hopes that I shall see His face with joy, that all my sins are pardoned, that my soul is accepted, that I am one who belongs to His eternal election, one whom He has separated for good. I hope I am one who shall have the fruit of all the purchase of the blood of Jesus Christ, that I shall live forever with God to enjoy communion with Him, that I shall be with Christ in His Kingdom to all eternity, and have a crown of glory incorruptible; that I shall join with saints and angels to be eternally blessing and praising God in the highest heavens. I have hopes of such things as these are."

Certainly the greatness of the hopes of the saints, has a great deal of efficacy in it to purge the heart, and that upon these grounds, because the hopes are hopes of such great things. Titus 2:11–13 shows that the greatness of the hope of the saints causes them to purge themselves from the filth of sin: "For the grace of God that bringeth salvation hath appeared to all men, teaching us that denying ungodliness and worldly lusts, we should live soberly, righteously, and godly in this present world, looking for that blessed hope, and the glorious appearing of the great God and our Savior Jesus Christ." The grace of God has appeared; and what does it teach us? "To deny ungodliness and worldly lusts, and to live soberly, righteously, and godly in this imperfect world," not to reserve our godliness for the world to come. And what's the ground of this? "Looking for that blessed hope, and the glorious appearing of the great God and our Savior Jesus Christ."

These particulars show that the greatness of the

hopes of the saints is that which causes them to purify themselves:

PARTICULAR 1. The hopes of the saints are so great, such things as indeed (were they not revealed in the Word would be blasphemy to hope for) that ever such a creature should come to enjoy so much as this hope raises up the heart to expect from God.

It first elevates the heart, because the things are so high that the soul hopes for; the heart of a man or woman, before God puts in these hopes, lies groveling upon the ground, and even the curse of the serpent is upon such a one (upon his belly he goes, and dust he eats, he knows no other things than these that are in the world, and therefore his heart closes with them). But these hopes elevate and raise the heart on high, because the things are high. Men who are busied with lofty things scorn the baseness that there is in lesser things. Men who are busied about high state affairs in the nation scorn the sordidness in other men whose business is altogether about low and mean things. Commonly men's spirits are according to the objects that they are busied about. Those kinds of people, who have no other objects to be busied about but scraping dustheaps and gutters, have low spirits; but men who are bred in other things, as in the knowledge of the heavens, or state affairs, have spirits elevated accordingly.

The hopes of the saints, being such great and glorious things, elevate the spirits of the children of God, and make them scorn baseness. Sin is baseness, and of all things in the world their hearts must be above sin. The greatest baseness in the world is that which carnal hearts account their chief good. The saints scorn that which is below them and under them; there is in the hearts of the saints a holy kind of elevation of spirit that God loves, that is, that they should think themselves too good for those base, low, and sordid things that the men of the world take delight in. Surely a man would think it a very sad thing to have his child love to be among swine in the pig's sty, and be flapping with them in the swill tub. A man who is of any worth would account it a great affliction to have his child of such a low spirit, but he would have him of a higher nature, and to scorn that. So the hopes of the saints put an ingenious spirit into that which is suitable to the things that he hopes for.

Ambrose reports that Theodosa, a godly and gracious virgin, being put upon to sacrifice to the idol gods, refused to do so. The judges, to invent some kind of torment to force her to do it, could think of nothing that would more provoke her than this, to condemn her to live in a brothel, and so have her body abused there; that was the judgment that they would condemn her to, for that, they thought, would prevail with her above anything. And when she was to go here, and some others likewise with her, they made a great fire, and put it to their choice, either to be cast into this fire or to go to the brothel. When they saw it, they freely leaped into the fire rather than to go to that place of uncleanness. Thus you see what spirits the people of God have, how much they are above that which the world accounts happiness. Many filthy, unclean, wretched hearts will venture the loss of God, and all to satisfy the flesh in the uncleanness; they think it the greatest joy and contentment that they can have to satisfy the flesh in filthiness and uncleanness if they might have liberty. But see the spirits of these: they account that the greatest misery, for their hearts were elevated above such base things. That is the first thing: the greatness of the hopes of the saints elevates and raises them higher above the baseness of sin.

PARTICULAR 2. Because the hopes of the saints are

such great things, therefore they must be jealous and fearful of everything that in any way may contradict their hopes, because their hopes are hopes of such high and great things as they are indeed. The hopes of carnal hearts are low and mean things, and therefore they are not so fearful and jealous of that which may hinder them, because they do not see the reality of such blessed and glorious things as the saints do. But now when hoping for a kingdom, glory, immortality, eternal communion with Father, Son, and Holy Spirit in the highest heavens, certainly any thing in the world that may be a crossing to this hope, the hearts of the saints must rise against. Now sin in its own nature is such as would deprive the saints of the enjoyment of these hopes; howsoever, through the strength of the covenant of grace, God carries them on, so that they shall not utterly be deprived, but yet they see that sin of its own nature would undo them.

PARTICULAR 3. The greatness of their hopes fills their hearts with so much comfort and satisfaction, their souls are so satisfied with the good that they hope for, that they account they have enough and need not look to any other thing for comfort and contentment. They have enough in their own hearts; their hope fills their souls with joy unspeakable and glorious. What is the reason why carnal hearts seek up and down for comfort in this and the other lust? It is because they do not have enough in God. But the saints have the spring of consolation within through these hopes; these hopes fill them with so much comfort that the temptation that would draw them to sin has no power to prevail against them; for where lies the power of a temptation to sin but in that it offers some contentment that the heart did not have before? And therefore people who are discontent are subject to temptation. You do not know how liable you make yourselves to temptations when you are discontent and lack comfort within. When the devil sees such a one, he says, "Here is an object fit for me; he lacks comfort. Now I will go and present some comfort to him, for he is vexed and troubled. And I may draw him to such and such an evil way."

No people are in more danger of temptations than melancholy and discontented persons, for the strength of a temptation lies in offering some contentment that we lack. Now if the heart is filled with comfort, and spiritual and heavenly things, so that I find my soul fully satisfied and quieted, I can say, "Return unto your rest, O my soul, for the Lord has dealt bountifully with me. Whatsoever I lack in the creature, I have the light of the face of God; and I know I have enough laid up in God, Christ, heaven, the covenant, and the promises."

Now the devil sees that there is little hope of prevailing with such a soul to draw it to sin. He thinks with himself, "How can I offer contentment to them? Their hearts are satisfied with better contentment than I can offer to them!" The reason a temptation prevails is because the devil thinks that he has better comforts and contentment than you have in your own hearts; but the devil, the world, and the flesh (put them all together) cannot offer better and sweeter comforts than this hope in the hearts of the saints fills them with. Hence it is that the greatness of the hopes of the saints helps to purge and keep the heart from sin, because they fill the heart with so much joy and comfort.

If a man should have his body filled with sweet wines, if you should come now to offer him a small beer, do you think you could prevail with him to drink it? The saints have the rich wine of heavenly consolation, and they fill themselves through the hopes that they have in those great things of the gospel. They fill their hearts with the rich wine of the consolation of the Spirit of God, and that which the devil, the world, or the flesh offer is but a little sapless stuff, dead beer, after they are so filled with other comforts.

PARTICULAR 4. The greatness of the hope of the saints purges their hearts because it enflames their spirits with love for God. "Oh, that ever God should look upon such a worm, a vile wretch in myself, a child of wrath and an heir of hell who might have been fuel for the anger of the infinite God to have burned upon to all eternity; that God should raise up my condition as He has done, and given me hope; and not vain hopes, but grounded hopes of enjoyment of such glorious and blessed things! Oh, what shall I render to the Lord!" The love of Christ must constrain such a heart. Now when a temptation to sin comes, the heart says, "What, shall I do such a thing and sin against such a God, who has raised me from the gulf of despair, and given me the hope of that glorious Kingdom that He has provided for His saints? Shall I sin against this God?"

Oh, these hopes enflame the heart with love for God, and nothing can purify the heart from sin more than the love of God. The love of God in Jesus Christ is a mighty, purging thing. We know that fire purges and cleanses, and the love of God is hot in the heart; it is as a fire in the very bones. Oh, it purifies the heart from the dross that before was in it. The love of God is shed abroad in the soul, and nothing in the world cleanses as that does. That's the first ground of purifying the heart by these hopes, because they are such great hopes. And therefore he who has this hope purifies himself.

Chapter 15

*The Saints Purify Themselves Because Their
Hopes Usually Cost Them Dearly*

PARTICULAR 5. He who has this hope purifies him-self because his hopes cost him dearly. The hopes of the saints usually cost them dearly, and therefore they are loathe to lose them. They are careful to maintain them, knowing how dearly they cost them. Sometimes God even sanctifies from the womb, and so by degrees raises the heart to hope, but even these find it costs them dearly to maintain their hopes; ordinarily it costs them dearly to both get them and maintain them. It costs them a great deal of humiliation; it costs them many prayers and tears, taking many pains, and much searching the Word and the covenant of grace. It is only after a long time that their hearts are somewhat raised with hope.

Those who for the most part have these hopes can remember what a sad condition they were in before they had them, when their hearts were despairing, and what a great deal of labor, pains, and cost they ex-pended before their hearts were raised with these hopes. And when they have gotten them with much dif-ficulty and pains, they think, "Shall I lose them for nothing?" Any of you who are of the poorer sort, who get your daily bread by the sweat of your brows, if you have labored and toiled a long time, and it may be have gotten ten or twenty shillings together by laying aside now a groat, and then sixpence, perhaps you have scraped a little money together—how careful are you in preserving that little? You will not lose what you have gotten with a great deal of pain, and labor for a trifle. Now the saints get what they have with labor and cost, and hence it is that they are so careful to preserve it. And therefore, because they see that the filth and defilement of sin would hinder their hopes and take away the comfort they bring, therefore they fight so much against their sin; whereas the hopes of the greatest part of the world are things that lightly come and lightly go; they cost them nothing.

I appeal to you, what do your hopes cost you? What pains did you take before you attained to these hopes? For this is certain, all men and women in the world are the children of wrath by nature; therefore the hopes that are hopes of a right stamp usually cost you dearly. But you who neither know what they cost you, nor how they are to be maintained, it is no wonder therefore if you can lose the comforts of your hopes, and if they do not purge your hearts, if your hopes may stand with the way of sin and wickedness. Because your hopes are such light things, you easily get them, and so you can easily part with them. You can commit sin, and still you hope that the Lord will be merciful unto you, and so you sin again and hope again. Your hopes come lightly, and go lightly away.

But the saints get their hopes by prayer and watchfulness, care, examination of their hearts and the Word; and if at any time they fall into sin, they lose the comfort and the sense of their hope, and then they are fain to seek again, as if they were new to begin. And then they think, "When was there ever any who had true grace who has fallen as I have done?" And so they are many times in their own apprehension forced to begin all afresh.

Now when they see what their sins put them to, and how it eclipses or obscures their hopes, and cost them so dearly, this makes them heed what they do. In Ezra 9:8, that holy man makes this argument: "And now for a little space grace hath been shewed from the Lord our God, to leave us a remnant to escape, and to give us a nail in his holy place, that our God may lighten our eyes and give us a little reviving in our bondage." And then verse 14: "Should we again break Thy commandments?" He speaks upon the strength of what he said in verse 8. It is as if Ezra had said, "Oh, Lord, we were in great bondage, and it was a mighty work of Thine ever to deliver us so far as we are delivered, to give us a nail in Thy holy place, and a little reviving in our bondage. And Lord, shall we again forsake Thee and break Thy commandments?"

This is an ingenious kind of arguing. Just so is the arguing of a gracious heart about his hope: "Oh, Lord God, I who was in bondage, who had the spirit of bondage upon me, saw myself as a bond slave to sin and to the devil. And now, Lord, hast Thou, by Thine almighty power, and by Thine infinite grace and mercy, given me a little hope that Thou dost intend good unto me in Jesus Christ, will save this soul of mine, and bring me to heaven and eternal life? Should I again forsake Thee, and break Thy commandments then? Should I again return to those former sins I lived in that cost me so dearly, that made such a breach between the infinite God and my soul, when the Lord has been pleased to deliver me, and given me such hope? Was there not a time that I would have given ten thousand worlds, if I had had them, to raise my heart from the gulf of despair that I saw myself sinking into? And has the Lord been pleased to give unto me a little reviving, and shall I again break the commandments?"

An ingenious, gracious heart makes use of this strong argument from the hope that God gives unto him, the little reviving that God gives unto him, because the Lord had given it with much difficulty. It was a wonderful work of God ever to raise him to these hopes; and indeed, one who has this hope admires God's infinite mercy, that He has been pleased to make such an alteration in his condition. "Oh, that such a one as I was is able to look upon the face of the infinite and just God with hope, to smile at death, the king of terrors, and to expect the great day of judgment with hope!" Oh, he admires God's grace in it, and therefore he is loath to lose the comfort of it. Hence he comes to purge himself. He has from hence a strong argument against every kind of sin whatsoever.

Chapter 16

*The Saints Purify Themselves Because
Their Hope Is a Scripture Hope*

PARTICULAR 6. The hope of one who is godly purges from sin because it is a Scripture hope. When the saints hope in God, they do not hope in a confused way; they do not build their hopes upon the sand, but they look into the Word of God and build their hopes upon Scripture. Hence it must follow that therefore their hopes must be according to the tenor of Scripture, and, if they are so, they must be purging hopes. That they build their hopes upon the Scripture is evident from Psalm 119:41: "Let Thy mercies come also unto me, O Lord, even Thy salvation, according to Thy Word." It is as if David should say, "O Lord, for my part I never expect mercy nor salvation, but only according to Thy Word. I never look for it upon any other terms, but merely according to Thy Word. Let me have Thy mercy and Thy salvation according to Thy promise, and not otherwise. If Thy Word will not give it to me, if I do not have it upon the terms of Thy Word, Lord, I am content to be without it."

I put this to every one of you, and desire that you would make use of this in your own consciences. See whether you have David's spirit or not: "Lord, I hear out of Thy Word such and such things upon such and such terms. Thou hast promised mercy to people who are thus and thus. Lord God, I am content to venture my soul upon that, never to look upon Thy face with any expectation of mercy but only as the Word shall bear me out in it. And if Thy Word shall not encourage me, let me not have it." Verse 81 of this psalm: "My soul fainteth for Thy salvation, but I hope in Thy Word." Still it is the Word that is the ground of the hopes of the saints. Romans 15:4: "Whatsoever things were written aforetime were written for our learning, that we, through patience and comfort of the Scriptures, might have hope." So the hopes of the saints are Scripture hopes.

Therefore it follows that these hopes must be purging hopes, because the Scripture holds forth no ground of hope but upon such terms of purging and purifying them. Therefore in Isaiah 1:16–18, the ground for the hopes of mercy are held forth: "Wash you, make you clean; put away the evil of your doings from before Mine eyes; cease to do evil; learn to do well; seek judgment, relieve the oppressed, judge the fatherless, plead for the widow. Come now, and let us reason together . . . though your sins be as scarlet, they shall be as white as snow; though they be red like crimson, they shall be as wool." Observe that God will not so much as discuss the case with any sinner for doing away with their sins till they resolve to wash and make themselves clean, to put away the evil of their doings, and to cease to do evil. "Come now, and let us reason together," says God, "there is no thought that you should have any hope of any mercy from Me till you are willing to put away the evil of your doings from before My eyes."

Certainly, though, we cannot say that before the soul closes with God's mercy in Christ there is an actual sanctification. Yet we may say that before the soul has any grounded hope that God should put away his sins, there must be washing; there must be making clean, putting away the evil of their doings, ceasing to do evil, and learning to do well. This is the Scripture way of raising the hope of the saints. If we would reason the case with God, we must come with such resolutions. Indeed when the soul first believes, it comes to Christ to wash away the evil of sin as well as to wash away the guilt of sin. If it is a Scripture hope, it must be a purging hope.

Upon this ground, those who have this hope purge themselves, because grounding their hopes upon the Scriptures they find that the tenor of the Scripture runs so. They who will have the blessing of the covenant of grace must be sanctified. So in Jeremiah 31:33, how does the tenor of the covenant of grace run there? "This shall be the covenant that I will make with the house of Israel: After those days I will put My law in their inward parts, and write it in their hearts; and I will be their God, and they shall be My people."

Have you hopes that God will be your God? The terms upon which this goes, and the tenor of this covenant is that God will "write His law in their inward parts." What's that? He will give you a gracious frame of spirit, so that there shall be an inward sympathy between your hearts and whatsoever is written in the law of God; there shall be a disposition in your hearts suitable to what is written in God's law. Whenever God enters into covenant with your soul, He does this. If your hopes are according to what is written in the Scripture, they must be cleansing and purifying hopes.

The truth is, the Scriptures dash the hopes of the wicked and ungodly. Read Romans 1:18: "For the wrath of God is revealed from heaven against all ungodliness." What do you say to this Scripture? Will your hopes stand with this Scripture? In 1 Corinthians 6:9, you have reckoned up a great many several sorts of sinners; and none of all these shall enter into the kingdom of heaven. Romans 8:13: "For if ye live after the flesh, ye shall die." He who seeks to satisfy the flesh and the lusts of the flesh shall perish. Will your hopes stand with this Scripture, yes or no? Hebrews 12:14: "Follow peace with all men, and holiness, without which no man shall see the Lord." Can your hopes stand with that Scripture?

It's certain the hopes of the saints may stand with every Scripture, with every verse in all the Book of God. You will say, "Some Scriptures speak terribly to me, but others speak comfortably." But if your hopes are right, they may stand with every line and word. There's nothing in all the Book of God that is against your hopes. This is a certain truth, that if it shall prove at the day of judgment that there is but one verse in all the Book of God against your hopes, you are undone forever. Consider this thing and lay it up: If when your hopes of eternal life come to be examined at the great day, there is found but one verse in all the Book of God against your hopes, you are a lost and undone man or woman forever. Whatever conceits you had before that all might be well with you, whatsoever other people thought of you, yet one Scripture at the great day will cast you out forever. Your hopes must be Scripture hopes; they must be according to the tenor and way of the Scripture, and therefore they must be purging hopes.

Chapter 17

Four Additional Grounds of the Saints' Hope

PARTICULAR 7. The hopes of the saints must be purging because they are lively hopes. 1 Peter 1:3 says that we are begotten to "a lively hope." It is always living, and therefore working. How does the liveliness of the hopes of the saints appear but by working out corruptions? How does a fountain appear to be living but by continually working? Nothing more lively expresses the difference between the sins of the saints and the sins of the wicked men as dirt in water on the highway and dirt cast into a living spring. So the hopes of the saints are lively, not only living but lively. A man may be a living man, but not lively; but the hopes of the saints are both living hopes and lively hopes. Living hopes are part of the new nature, the Spirit of life that God does put into the soul, which is in Scripture called the life of God, and therefore is very active and stirring. So they are not only part of that life, but lively hopes that have continual matter to quicken and feed them; and it is the care of the saints to be feeding their hopes, and to keep them in a living plight, because the very joy of their lives depends upon their hopes. Continual action and stirring keeps from corruption; the hopes of the saints are lively, but the hopes of the wicked are dead, dull kinds of hopes, and therefore may stand with their corruptions.

PARTICULAR 8. The hopes of the saints must be purifying hopes because they are pitched upon God and Jesus Christ. I could give you many Scriptures for their pitching upon God, Psalm 78:7–8, and 1 Peter 1:21–22. I need not recite the words, but their hopes are pitched upon God. In 1 Timothy 1:1, Christ is our hope, and all hope is pitched upon Him. Those hopes that are pitched upon God, whereby the soul converses much with God and Jesus Christ, must purify. The more any heart acts upon God and Christ, and converses with them, they must have their hearts very pure. You complain of your corruptions, and a great deal of filthiness abides still in you. Would you know the way to purge your hearts? Let your spirits be much exercised with God and Jesus Christ. When a gracious heart has been with God in meditation, or in any holy duty, and has found the ability to raise the heart to communion with God and Jesus Christ, it comes from those duties with mighty, strong resolutions against sin, and it can come wonderfully cleansed from the drossiness of the spirits that they had before they so conversed with God and Christ.

When Moses was in the mountain and conversed with God, he came down with his face shining. Why? Because he had been conversing much with God. So those who converse much with God have shining hearts and shining conversations. The reason for the dullness and drowsiness of your hearts and conversations is because you converse much with the world; but conversing with God and Christ, the holy One of God, will cleanse and purify your hearts. Job 11:14–15: "If iniquity be in thine hand, put it far away, and let not wickedness dwell in thy tabernacles, for then shalt thou lift up thy face without spot." You cannot lift up your face without spot, fear, and trembling unless iniquity is put far away from you. The man who would have a free heart converse with God, who would lift up his face to God with joy, and would have a steadfast heart without fear, if he has iniquity in his hand he must put it away, and not let wickedness dwell in his tabernacle. Those two cannot stand together. If there is any wickedness in your house; if you would not lose your freedom in your conversation with God, put the wickedness away, for He cannot stand both together. So the hopes of the saints purge out wickedness because, by their hopes, they converse so much with God and Christ, and are acting so much upon them. Hence it is that they do purge and cleanse their hearts.

Further, the hopes of the saints are hopes in the Holy Ghost, as in Romans 15:13, where we are said to be filled with hope by the power of the Holy Ghost.

Again, you heard before that the hopes of the saints are grounded upon faith, and faith purifies the heart. Hope is the daughter of faith, and therefore has the efficacy of faith in it. Those things were before, but these things show where the influence of this purifying quality of hope is, because it is wrought by the power of the Holy Ghost and has its ground in faith.

PARTICULAR 9. The saints purify themselves because the things hoped for are such pure and holy things. If we consider what are the holy things that the soul hopes for, they are things so holy and pure that it cannot be but that the hopes of such things must purify the heart. I need go no further than the very verse before our text: "Now we are the sons of God, and it doth not yet appear what we shall be; but we know when He shall appear, we shall be like Him, for we shall see Him as He is. And every man that hath this hope in Him, purifies himself, even as He is pure." What hope is the apostle speaking of? The hope that when Jesus Christ shall appear we shall be like Him, and shall see Him as He is. Oh, one day I shall be like Jesus Christ; the great thing that I hope for! It is not so much that I shall forever be freed from hell and the unspeakable torments of the damned; but this I hope, that though I have a wretched heart of my own, yet I hope one day I shall be made like Jesus Christ Himself. I shall see Jesus Christ as He is in all His holiness and all His glory. I hope for this. Certainly if these are the things that I hope for, then my labors must be suitable to being as much like Christ as I can. If people understood what they mean when they say they hope to go to heaven, it could not but cause them to purge themselves from sin and wickedness. You hope to go to heaven, but what do you hope for in heaven? Truly you want to be happy and glorious, but what does that mean? If God has acquainted your soul with true hope, your true happiness will be that you shall be forever in heaven with Jesus Christ and be like Him. You shall see Him in His holiness and glory. That is what you hope for; that is the happiness of heaven that you should rejoice in every time you think of it.

Certainly, if you rejoice in this hope, then your soul should labor to be as much like Christ as it can be. That is what I should account to be the glory of heaven to my soul. Certainly, if your heart is in heaven, you will be glad to have as much of heaven here on earth as you can for the present.

PARTICULAR 10. Surely he who has this hope must purge himself, because the purging of the soul is but a preparation for the enjoyment of all the good a gracious heart hopes for. Now if it hopes for it, it must follow that it will labor to prepare for what it hopes for. Suppose that two persons were betrothed; if the engagement is broken, and there are few hopes that the marriage will go on, they never trouble themselves about preparing for it. But when there is a match, and it begins to go on hopefully, when they are fully persuaded that it will proceed, and they expect the very day when the solemnization shall be, then they begin to think of preparation, of their clothes, of their friends, and where they should hold the marriage feast. They begin to prepare once they are sure that the wedding will go on, and the date is set.

This is the difference between those who are carnal and those who are spiritual. You who are carnal hear of Christ, and of a match between the soul and Christ in general. But regarding those who are spiritual, the Holy Spirit comes and not only reveals such a thing in general, but comes and persuades the soul, though very poor and wretched in itself, as thus: "God the Father intends His Son to be a match for you, and it is determined in heaven that you are the soul that shall enjoy Jesus Christ as your Husband for all eternity. The glory of Jesus Christ shall be upon you, and the time is appointed when Jesus Christ shall come with all His glory for the full solemnity of this match. He will take your soul and body to Himself to live for evermore with Him in those mansions which He has gone to prepare."

Now when the soul comes first to believe this and, believing this, comes to have hope raised, and hopes for that day coming, the soul thinks, "What must I do to prepare myself then for this Bridegroom? How shall I fit myself for this day of the coming of Jesus Christ?" It is indeed as excellent a sign of true grace as any one I know of when the heart is taken off from other things, and now has such a clear manifestation of Christ, and such faith and hope in Christ, and of the part that it shall have in Christ, and communion with Him—the great care and work of such a soul in the whole course of its life here is nothing else but to prepare itself for the meeting of the Bridegroom, to meet with Jesus Christ, and so to meet with Him as to enjoy everlasting communion with Him. Before this his thoughts and cares were about this and the other thing in the world, to make provision for himself. Yet now the strength of his soul is spent upon the great work of preparing his soul to meet with Jesus Christ when He comes. Now he thinks like this: "My desire is to be presented blameless before Him at His coming, whenever it shall be. I have hopes of this glorious match. The great day of judgment, that shall be the day of horror and vexation of ungodly and wicked men, shall be the day of the glorious match of my soul to Christ. And therefore what is the course of my life and the care of my heart but to prepare my soul for this time? Other men and women may be busied about this and the other business, but the work that I have to do is to prepare my soul for the coming of Jesus Christ, that I expect to behold, and to be made like Him."

Now, can this stand with living in any way of known sin? It's impossible but where there are such things as these are, such a soul must purify himself as He is pure.

Chapter 18

The Application

USE 1. Certainly, then, those hopes are to be reproved that are so far from purging from sin that they are the great nourishers of sin. They are abominable hopes, and those are therefore wicked who have so much hope. If they did not believe that God were as merciful as He is, they would be more careful of their lives than they are. Now this is a desperate kind of believing, for men to be the more wicked because they believe God is the more merciful; and yet I dare appeal to most people, if you thought that God were not as merciful as He is; if you believed that God were more severe than indeed you do believe, would you not be more careful of your ways? We see by experience that at such times when men have least hopes, that is, upon the sickbed or death bed, when the very ice is cracking and they are ready to be swallowed up by the gulf of eternal misery, then they would be godly and would purge themselves. But when they have health, peace, and some hope, now they are ungodly.

So the best condition that many people are in is when they are most in despair, when they are ready to die, when their hopes are most shaken—then are they in the best tune. But it is otherwise with the saints: when their hopes are most raised, then their hearts are most sanctified; and that is an excellent sign. It is as good a sign of grace as any when you can say, "Blessed be God! When my hopes are most raised, then is my heart most sanctified." The Scripture speaks an abundance of peace and comfort to such a soul.

USE 2. If such hopes purify, hence we have warrant to labor to get the hearts of the most vile sinners in the world to believe, and so to get hope of God's mercy. We have warrant to open the treasures of grace to the vilest sinners in the world, and to labor to draw their hearts at the very first to Jesus Christ, and to these hopes, because the very hopes will purge as much as anything. We can never use any means to purge their hearts as much as by showing them the grace of God that they may hope in.

OBJECTION. But you will say, "Hope cannot live with sin and corruption."

ANSWER. No, but the way to get the soul from sin and corruption is to manifest the Object of this glorious hope of the saints to the soul. The very first work that shall draw the heart to believe and hope in Jesus Christ will draw the heart from the love of every sin and corruption whatsoever.

USE 3. The saints have great temptations and discouragements because there is much sin and corruption in their hearts. They think that therefore it is presumption for them to hope because their corruptions are so great. This point may help against that temptation. Certainly, it is not presumption for you to believe and hope if it purges your heart. Why are you afraid that it is presumption? "Oh, because I have such a naughty and vile heart; therefore it is presumption for me to hope."

But I can say, because you hope that you shall not have so naughty a heart, certainly it is as pleasing to God that we should have a better heart by hoping as well as have a better heart and then hope. Yea, it is more evangelical to have a purged heart by hoping than to hope because I have a purged heart. In the other you go on in a more legal way. You then say, "I'll first hope, and then my hope shall purge me." Oh, go that way to understand hope, and then you will find as much and more comfort in that way than in the other.

USE 4. How this cuts the sinews of almost all false hope, for they neither are purged, nor do they hope, and so are purged. They are neither purged before or after hope. And when it is neither, then certainly those hopes can never do good to the soul in the day of Jesus Christ. The Scripture compares the hopes of the wicked to the spider's web in Job 8:14. A spider takes a great deal of pains in making a web, and then comes the broom of the maid and in one dash takes it all away. So there are many people who spin out their hopes out of themselves, as the spider does, and not out of the Word, nor out of the bowels of Jesus Christ, but out of themselves. From their good meanings, their good actions, their good serving of God, a fine web is made; but when the broom of death comes, all is dashed.

When a wicked man dies, his hopes perish (Proverbs 11:7). In Job 14:19, the hopes of the wicked are compared to a thing that grows out of the dust; and indeed the hopes of wicked men grow out of the very dust. They do not grow out of the Word or the covenant of grace, but out of the dust; and therefore they quickly vanish and come to nothing. These two are joined together in Ephesians 2:12: "Without God, and without hope." Certainly an abundance of people live without God in the world, and yet they will say that they have hope! But if you are without God in the world, then certainly you are without hope, without this true saving hope. Now the hopes, therefore, of most people in the world are vanishing things and will come to nothing.

For they hope, but their hope is a mere contradiction. Suppose a man should go into his plowed field and sow tares in the field. "Well," says he, "I hope I shall have as good a crop of wheat as any man in all the country." Would not any man in the world think that man mad who should hope for wheat when he sowed tares? Certainly the hopes of heaven and eternal life in most people are as foolish and contradictory in themselves as this kind of hope. What do you sow in your life? You sow nothing but wickedness in the course of your life, and yet you hope for heaven, glory, immortality, and the like; when the Scripture tells you plainly, "As a man soweth, so shall he reap."

There is a most wicked presumption in your hope if you go on in sin. There is an impious, wicked presumption in your hope, and it provokes God exceedingly against the soul. He cannot but look with indignation upon such a heart as vile and wretched, and He will cast you off one day with indignation.

If a man should come to me and say, "Sir, I depend upon you to help in such a business, and I am undone if you do not help me; for all my expectation is upon you." Presently I will direct him in a way that he should go. Now if he goes quite contrary to what I gave him directions about, and yet says that he hopes I will help him, would not any man account himself mocked in this case? Truly in this manner wicked and ungodly men mock God to His very face.

God protests, in the most solemn manner that is possible for any to protest, that such and such who do certain things shall never inherit the kingdom of heaven. Hope and hope as much as you will, yet if there is a God you shall perish. And yet one still says, "I hope that God will not do as He says." You dare not say so openly, but in effect you do; in your hearts you say so. This is mocking God to His very face. But God will not be mocked.

And know, there's a great deal more evil in vain hopes than you are aware of. It dishonors God in His holiness. It is apparent that you do not know as yet what an infinitely holy God you have to deal with. God takes this extremely ill at your hands, and looks upon this wickedness of your heart with indignation, that you would dare flatter yourself with such hopes when the Word of God in such a solemn manner detests it.

This hope of yours is quite contrary to all the plot of God in His election, in the work of redemption. What was the great plot in His election? He has chosen us that we might be a holy people unto Him. Now if you think, "I hope that God intends good to me," and yet go on in wickedness, you cross the plot of God's election.

The same is true of redemption: He has purchased us to Himself that we might be zealous of good works. He redeemed us from the hands of our enemies so that we might serve Him in holiness all the days of our lives. It is the very compact between God the Father and God the Son that such as are redeemed should be redeemed so that they might be holy to God. If you hope that you are one of God's elect ones, and are a redeemed one of God, if you go on in sin, you cross the very design that God had in the work of election and in the work of redemption. Love of sin and hope in God's mercy cannot stand together.

Chapter 19

An Exhortation To Put Away Sin

If your hopes cannot stand without purifying yourself and laboring for the greatest exactness in order to be pure as Christ is pure; if they can stand with walking in the way of sin, of filthiness and corruption, oh, then, away with your sin! Will you yet dare, after the knowledge of all this, to please yourself in any way of wickedness? Shall not your heart from this day forward be set against every false way?

Rather, should your heart not say, "Well, the Lord forbid that there should be any one beloved sin that I should entertain again; for the time to come it shall be the uttermost degree of strictness and holiness that I will endeavor after, even to purify myself as Jesus Christ is pure, for I have read that there can be no hopes of heaven and eternal life without purifying myself, and endeavoring to purify myself even as Jesus Christ is pure. I will never cry out of strictness, preciseness, and Puritanism again, but will set myself with all my power to imitate the pattern of Jesus Christ the Holy One." Will you go away with such resolutions as this? Oh, blessed be God then that ever you lived to hear or read this point. And there's a great deal of strength in it to cause you to cast away your beloved sins with indignation, and even say, "Get away! What have I to do any more with this idol, this lust, or that corruption?" Otherwise they will disappoint you of all your hope of eternal life.

If you had a dear friend who was willing to set you

up in trading, and told you that whatever you might need you could come to him for; but if he should say to you, "I require this at your hands: do not keep company with such a fellow. If you keep company with him, you shall never see my face." Would this not persuade you to cast off the company of anyone, if you had such a friend who might enrich you? In the same manner, you hope to have all the riches that there are in God Himself that you are capable of receiving, and God is willing to bestow them upon you. But He says, "Do not keep company with such a one; do not let your heart entertain such a wicked lust as you find so suitable to your nature; for, if you do, you shall never see My face. You shall never see any good in me, nor in My Son." Now, will you yet venture upon any beloved sin? Is there so much good to be had in any corruptions as to countervail the loss of your hopes?

Truly, when I meditate upon this point, I see God, and even hear Him crying to wretched and wicked sinners who live in wickedness and wallow in their filthy lusts, "O wretched sinner, if ever you would have any part in Me, to have any good of all the riches that I have in heaven or earth, then cast away your beloved sin."

From this point Christ cries to sinners, "O wretched, sinful men and women, would you have any hope ever to enjoy any good in what I have purchased with My blood? If you have any hopes of enjoying it, cast away your sins; cast away your wickedness."

Your very souls are crying out to you, "Would you have us not perish eternally? Would you have us to have any hope of seeing the face of God with joy, and to have happiness when we are parted from this body? Then cast away such and such beloved corruptions; for our seeing the face of God with joy cannot stand with them."

The soul that after all this shall keep any way of

wickedness, any beloved sin still, how just would it be with God, with Jesus Christ, with the saints and angels, and their own consciences, to cry to have justice proclaimed against this soul! It is infinitely righteous that this man or woman should perish eternally, and one day it will be so. But when you hear that your hopes cannot stand without purging your souls and aiming at the uttermost purity, yet, if your hearts are so knit to the love of any base corruption that you will venture all: this will be the condition of every wicked man and woman who shall go on in wicked ways after reading these sermons. If you are so desperately wicked as to say, "In spite of all this, I'll venture to see whether the hopes of good in Christ and my lusts will not stand together," O devilish heart! You who dare to put a thing of such infinite consequence to the venture, if you do so, even the saints and angels, and your own conscience, shall echo forth to God, "Just art Thou O God, to sink such a soul into eternal despair, because he had such a love for his lusts as to risk his soul for them. And therefore it is just that he should be eternally sunk down into hideous darkness among damned spirits forevermore."

Now the Lord give you hearts to consider this while yet you are in the land of the living; for while we are alive, this is the time of raising our hopes. Whatever you are now, as long as the Lord gives you life there is a possibility to raise your hopes; but if God has cut you off in your sin, you are lost and undone forever. Consider therefore what the Lord preaches to you here, seeing that the hope of the saints about the glory of heaven is such a hope that whoever has it purifies himself, even as Jesus Christ is pure.

Appendix

The Misery of Those Who Have Their Portion in This Life

"From men of the world, who have their portion in this life." Psalm 17:14

This Psalm is David's moan unto God under Saul's persecution. Without a doubt, the psalmist aims at Saul in it; and in it we have these four things:

1. He appeals unto God to judge the righteousness of his heart towards Saul (verse 2): "Let my sentence come from Thy presence." From Saul and his courtiers there comes a hard sentence: They call me "traitor"; they call me "rebel"; but, Lord, leave me not unto their sentence. "Let my sentence come from Thy presence." That, I know, will be another sentence than what comes from them, for Thou hast proved me and tried me, and found nothing in me. That is the first thing.

2. He prays in verse 5 to God to keep him in his way, his going and his footsteps from sliding. "Lord, whenever the wrath of Saul is against me, yet let neither that, nor any other thing, put me out of Thy way; but keep my heart close unto Thee, and keep my paths in Thy way. Let not my footsteps so much as slide from Thee, for, Lord, they watch for my halting. If they can find but the least slip from me, they take advantage of it to the utmost. I am a poor and a weak creature; therefore, Lord help me that my footsteps may not slide."

3. He prays for deliverance (verse 7): "Show Thy mar-

velous lovingkindness to me." Lord, my straights are marvelous. I know not what to do to turn me, but my eyes are towards Thee. As straights are marvelous, so let the loving kindness of God be marvelous towards me, and keep me as the apple of Thine eye. O Lord, unto them I am but as a dog, a vile creature in the eyes of Saul, and those about him; but, blessed be Thy name, I can look up to Thee, and know that I am dear unto Thee as the apple of Thine eye.

All the saints of God are dear to God at all times, but the persecuted saints are the apple of God's eye. If at any time they are dear to God, they are especially dear when they are most persecuted. Not that they are the apple of His eye, and the apple of an eye is weak, and little able to resist any hurt, but so much the more is the man tender of the apple of his eye. The saints are weak and shiftless for themselves, but the Lord is so much the more tender over them. And one argument that the Psalmist uses in praying against his enemies is this (and a special one, because they prospered so much in this world): "they are enclosed in fat, and have their heart's desire, and Thou fillest their bellies with Thy hidden treasure. They leave to their babes; they have their portion in this life. Lord, keep me from them."

4. He professes his resolution, notwithstanding all the dangers he was in, to go on in the ways of God, and expects a gracious issue. "But I (said he) will behold Thy face in righteousness." Indeed I cannot behold the face of the King without danger to me. There are a great many that run to kill me, and they desire his face; but though I cannot see his face, yet, Lord, I shall behold Thy face. I will behold Thy face and it shall be in righteousness. I will still keep on in the ways of righteousness when I awake, for I believe that these troubles will not hold long. I shall not sleep in perpetual sleep, but I shall awake and be delivered; and then shall I be satisfied with Thy likeness. There shall be the manifestation of Thy glory to me; that

shall satisfy me for all the trouble that I have endured for Thy name's sake, that my soul shall say, 'I have enough.' " And this is the sum of this 17th Psalm. Now the words are read unto you; they are a description of David's adversaries, implying an argument why he would be delivered from them. They are described to be men of this world; they are only those that were adversaries to him, and a comfort it must be to the saints of God to see that none are their enemies but the men of this world, men of this world who have their portion in this life. They have something here, and here is all they are likely to have.

(1) It implies the argument why he would be delivered: "Lord, deliver me from them because they are men of this world who have their portion in their life." Therein consists the force of this argument; there lies the force of this argument, that he would be delivered from them because they were men of this world who have their portion in this life. It consists, first, in this: "Lord, they care not what injustice they do; they have no regard to anything but what is in this world. Therefore, be it right or wrong, may they have but their lusts in this world. That is all they care for. Lord, deliver me from such men."

(2) Here is all their good, their portion in this life; and, therefore, they are greedy upon this, let it be the ruin of never so many men. Though it is to raise their estates by my ruin, and the ruin of others that are never so innocent, what do they care? They are greedy upon having their lusts satisfied, for here is all their portion.

(3) Their portion is here is this world. They do not care for religion; they will make use of pretenses of religion any way for their own ends. What do they care what protestation they make for religion, and the maintenance of it, so be it that they may ruin me. They regard not at all anything in regard to have their own ends. Lord, deliver me from such men.

(4) They have their portion in the world; hence it

is that their hearts are so swelled with pride in their lusts, and so warm is their malice, so heated with such outrages. O let not the foot of pride come upon me! Deliver me from proud men that are flushed with the enjoyment of their heart's desires.

(5) They look only to what they enjoy in this world and, therefore, so long as they may have their own ends and lusts, they will be exceedingly hardened in their own ways. They will give no glory to Thee, but will be so much the more enraged against me by taking it as an argument that their ways are good. Lord, therefore, deliver me from those men.

(6) They are men who scorn at prayer, or at anything that is said concerning the tenderness of conscience. They despise conscience and prayer. Lord, let me never fall into the hands of such men as those are. Deliver me from the men of this world who have their portion in this life.

For the opening of the words "from the men of the world," the words are translated by some "from mortal men," from men though of the world, yet are not likely to enjoy the world long, for the original signifies as much from frail men, they shall not have it long, as in Psalm 89:47. Remember how short my time is; what little time I have in this world. The word is "from the men who shall have but a little time in this world, the men of this world" (the Hebrew word here, that is translated "men" sometimes, with but the change of the position of one prick, signifies "dead men," *mortui* as well as *vivi*). I say, with the change not of a pricked, but only of the position of one prick, of one point, it signifies dead men. They are men of the world, but such men as are within one prick of death, within one point of death, however they rejoice, who have their portion, their dimension that is given out unto them in this life. The word "life," though in the singular number in your books, in the Hebrew it is in the plural, "lives."

They are men who have all they have only leased for their lives; nay, not so much as leased, they have but an estate for life at the most, and this present life unto them is instead of all lives: from the men of this world who have their portion in this life.

There are these two doctrinal conclusions in the words that lie plainly before you.

DOCTRINE 1. There is a generation of men to whom God gives some outward good things for a while, but these are all that ever they are likely to have. They shall never have any more good from God than what they have here for the present.

DOCTRINE 2. God's saints desire to be delivered from such kinds of men.

These two doctrines contain in them the scope of the Holy Ghost in the words.

First, there is a generation of men unto whom God gives out a portion, some comforts in this world, and here is all that they are likely to have. And now set your hearts (I beseech you) unto what I have to say in this argument, for, in my thoughts, thinking what to pitch upon for such an assembly as this, at length I could not determine an argument that I thought might more reach unto the hearts of those to whom I was to speak. I hope (before I have done) you will find it such a serious argument that concerns us all. I have read of Gregory, who, being advanced to preferment, professed that there was no Scripture that went so to his heart, that struck such a trembling into his spirit, that daunted him so much, as this Scripture did. Here you have your reward: "Son, in your life time, you have had your pleasure." Oh, this was a dreadful Scripture that sounded in his ears continually! Jerome speaks of that Scripture, "Arise, you dead, and come to judgment." Night and day he thought that Scripture sounded in his ears. So, Gregory, here you have your reward; in this life you have had your pleasure. This was the Scripture that night and day sounded in his ears. Oh, that it might please God to assist so far to speak out of this Scripture to you, that I might make this Scripture ring in your ears even when you lie upon your beds after the sermon is done; that yet you may think this Scripture rings in your ears.

Men of this world who have their portion in this life, if this Scripture should prove to be their portion in this life, if this Scripture should prove to be the portion of any one of you of the richest in this place, woe unto him that ever he was born, which I shall after make out more fully to you. But, you'll say, do you think to preach to men who have their portion here in this life? I fear I may meet with some whom it so nearly concerns, yet do not think that I have those thoughts of you all, for you shall find (before I have done) this Scripture will concern every one in this congregation; but yet be not, any of you, too ready to put off this from you, to think yourselves out of the danger of this Scripture, for it was spoken concerning Saul, and Saul might have (for all I know) as strong arguments of God's love to him as many of you (I fear) have this day.

(1) Saul was a man chosen immediately by God Himself to be the first king that ever was over his own people; and was not that a great favor?

(2) Saul, for his person, was one of the goodliest men that was among all Israel, higher from the shoulders to the head than any of them.

(3) For his endowments, he was a man whom God endowed with admirable gifts of government. He caused another spirit to come upon him. He was a man who, when he heard of his preferment, seemed to be very humble, judging himself unworthy of such a dignity. In 1 Samuel 9:21 he said in so many words, "Who am I, and what is my father's house, that I should be thus chosen?" And when he had been chosen, some who would reject him, children of Belial, notwithstanding God's honoring

him, yet would seek to cast dishonor upon him. Yet this Saul had mighty power over his spirit. He was a very meek and quiet man. In 1 Samuel 10:27 the text says that he held his peace when the children of Belial said, "What have we to do with him?"

(4) Though he was quiet in his own cause, yet he showed himself to have an excellent spirit of government in a public cause. He was full of anger when it was for the good of the people that he governed, though quiet in his own (1 Samuel 11:6). When he heard of a dishonor done to the people of Israel, the text says that his anger rose within him; an excellent pattern for all governors, for all in public places, to be very silent, quiet, and self-denying, putting up wrongs in their own cause, but to be full of zeal for the public cause; to reserve their spirits for a public good. There are many in public places who, when they are angered in their private cause, how full of spirit they are; and they spend their spirit there so much that they have no spirit at all when it comes to a public cause. Saul went beyond them in this. Further yet:

(5) Saul was one who was very troubled at the sin of the people against God. He not only had a spirit to vindicate a public wrong, but when he saw the people sin against God his heart was very troubled at their very sin, and seemed to be grieved for it. He was mighty solicitous and careful about preventing sin in the people. This you have in 1 Samuel 14:33. They told Saul there that the people had sinned in eating with blood. Upon this Saul shows himself displeased. "Come and do not sin against the Lord; roll a stone to me hither." He would see with his own eyes that they slayed the cattle, and they poured forth the blood that they might not sin against God in eating blood. This was his care.

(6) Saul was very careful to inquire of God what he should do in this business of great consequence. In 1 Samuel 14:37, we see that he would not go out till he

had first inquired of God, yea, more than all this.

(7) He was a man who had a very reverend esteem for the prophets of God. When Samuel came to him in 1 Samuel 15:13, Saul said to him, "Blessed be thou of the Lord." Yea, yet further than this:

(8) When Samuel showed him what his sin was, in 15:30, he came and confessed it before the people and said, "I have sinned, I have sinned against the Lord," merely at the conviction of one prophet. Yea, yet more than this:

(9) God seemed to be with Saul very much, and to show great respect unto him in order to make him an instrument of much good to Israel. He granted unto him as glorious a victory as ever man had in this world (for so we may call it); and if there is any outward thing in the world might be gathered as an argument of God's love, it would be such a remarkable victory as he had over his enemies. This victory you shall find in 1 Samuel 13:5, and so read on afterwards in that chapter and the next. You shall find there that the Philistines were risen up against him and Israel, and there were thirty thousand chariots of his adversaries, the Philistines, and six thousand horsemen, and people as the sand of the sea for multitude besides all this. Well, here was a mighty enemy!

What did Saul have? Here was, on one side, thirty thousand chariots; here were six thousand horsemen; here were people as the sand of the sea without number; and Saul had but six hundred with him at this time. Yea, and of those six hundred, there was not one of them who had a sword but Saul and Jonathan; for the Philistines were wise enough to disarm all the malignants (that they accounted so), and would not let so much as a blacksmith be among them. They would not only take away their arms, but they would look to them to see that they had no arms supplied unto them. That was the wisdom of the Philistines; yet we find (if you read afterwards) in the

Scripture that God was so far with Saul that He blessed him and gave him victory over all these. Besides all this:

(10) God blessed Saul with a very gracious child, a godly son of a sweet nature, Jonathan, which indeed, if any outward argument in the world might be an argument of God's love, that might be.

But now put all these things together, and yet here is the man who has his portion in this world. I now challenge that man, especially I challenge him who has certain evidence of a mighty work of God upon him in Christ, let him show me greater arguments of God's love to him than Saul might have done; and yet it proved to be Saul's portion that he should have his portion only in this world. God herein shows that His mercy is His own, and that He will let out His mercy as He pleases: "It is your Father's pleasure to give you the kingdom." The Father doles out the portion as He pleases unto His children. God will let the line of His mercy to go this far to one and there stop, and so far to another and there stop, and then come in a cross line again unto them. God so disposes of His mercy that there are some who shall have heaven and earth to be their portion, and their portion is blessed indeed. There are some who shall have earth but not heaven, and their portion is poor and mean and sad. There are others who shall have heaven but not earth, and their portion is good. And there are others who shall neither have heaven nor earth, and their portion (you'll say) is miserable indeed. God's mercy is His own to dispose of as He will. We read that Abraham, in Genesis 21:14, called for Ishmael and Hagar, and he gave them a piece of bread, a bottle of water, and sent them away. There's an end of them. So Jehoshaphat, in 2 Chronicles 21:3, gave his other son (says the text) gifts, but the kingdom he gave to Jehoram.

So God has people to whom He gives pieces of bread and bottles of water, yea, some to whom He gives great gifts in this world, but He keeps His inheritance for His

Isaac. He keeps the kingdom for Jehoram. Esau had his portion in this world, and such a portion as he thought to be a very good portion. In Genesis 33:9 we read, "Brother (said he), I have enough." Most rich men are complaining; they do not go as far as Esau, who had his portion and thought he had enough. Christ's auditors, in Luke 6:24, had their portion in this world, "Woe to you, here is your consolation" (said Christ unto them). O dreadful speech! Woe to this man; woe to these, here are their consolations. Dives had his portion in this world in Luke 16:25: "Son, remember in thy lifetime thou hadst thy pleasure; and thou hadst thy good things." They were your good things, those things that were measured out for you. You had them in your lifetime.

In the handling of this argument, I shall divide what I have to say into these six particulars that you may, every one of you, go all the more readily along with me.

1. Why it is that God will deal out something to wicked men in this world? Why shall they have any portion at all?

2. Their portion is confined to this life, and why so?

3. Some corollaries naturally flow from these two.

4. We shall consider the condition of these men who are such that have their portion in this world.

5. I shall endeavor to show unto you who are those men, to cull out of the congregation what that man or woman is who is likely to have their portion in this world.

6. I will conclude with words of exhortation to you all.

PARTICULAR 1. God gives even to wicked men a portion. He doles out something because:

1. They are all His creatures. Jehu said, concerning Jezebel, "Go, take away this cursed woman; show some respect unto her; let her not lie there in the streets but take her away, for she is the daughter of a king." So God says, "Well, though these are cursed, yet they are My creatures. They shall have some respect from Me; some good I'll communicate to them." Indeed, it is not an argument

strong enough that because you are God's creatures, therefore God should be merciful eternally to you; but it may be argument strong enough that, because you are His creatures, you shall have something.

2. This time of life is the time of patience, the day of God's longsuffering.

3. Therefore, you shall have something; and the day of patience is man's day. In 1 Corinthians 4:3, the apostle there says, "I pass not for man's judgment." The words are in the Greek "for man's day." The words may be translated, "I pass not for man's day." It is as if the apostle should say, "It is true, man carries all before him now; man has all the doings now at this day, and he may judge and censure as he pleases. It is but his day, and I pass not for man's day." The day of patience may prove to be man's day.

4. Wicked men do something for God here, some kind of service, that is at least materially a service for God. And God will not have them clamor upon Him that they have nothing for their work. God will give to everyone something for what they do for Him, though it is never so little here in this world. You have a famous place for that in Ezekiel 29:18–20. Nebuchadnezzar, King of Babylon, caused his army to serve a great service against Tyrus, yet had he no wages for his army (said God); he had no wages for his service. Well, therefore, God inquired about this, and seemed to complain that when Nebuchadnezzar did Him any service yet he should be all this while without his wages. Therefore (said God), "Behold! I will give the land of Egypt unto him; he shall take a spoil and a prey, and that shall be his wages." He will give him wages for what he does. God makes use of many wicked men in divers services, and His churches shall have much refreshing and good from them. The Lord causes the very earth to help the women and earthly men to be of use to the church, and God will not be beholding to them for their work. A

thorn may serve to stop a gap though it is but a thorn bush, and if it serves to stop a gap, and is of any use, it has that benefit by it. All that while it is kept from the fire, whereas, were it not of use, it might presently be brought to the fire.

This is an argument, by the way, to provoke all men to be of as much use to the church of God as they possibly can. It may be that is the very thing that keeps you from the fire. You are a thorn, but God has use of you and, therefore, does not bring you to the fire; but if you come to be un-useful, the fire is the next thing you shall hear of. I remember Augustine (in *The City of God*, Book 5, chapter 12) speaks of the Romans who had such a flourishing condition for a while, and he gives, for one reason, that the Romans had brave spirits. They were men who had excellent morals and heroic spirits, and were delivered from that baseness of spirit other people had. And, therefore, God showed some kind of respect unto them. Many instances of that kind might be given.

5. God gives wicked men a portion here to show unto them what little good there is in all these things, and to show the world what little good there is in all the things that are here below in the world. Certainly, if there were much good, they should never have them. It is an argument that there is no great excellency in the strength of body, for an ox has it more than you; an argument there is no great excellency in agility of body, for a dog has it more than you; an argument no great excellency in gay clothes, for a peacock has them more than you; an argument there is not any great excellency in gold and silver, for the Indians who know not God have them more than you. And, if these things had any great worth in them, certainly God would never give them to wicked men.

As it is a certain argument there is no great evil in afflictions in this world because the saints are so much afflicted, so it is no great argument that there is any great good in this world because the wicked enjoy so much of it. Luther had such an expression as this is in his commentary on Genesis. He said, "The Turkish Empire, as great as it is, is but a crumb that the master of the family, God, casts to dogs." That is all the esteem the whole Turkish Empire held for Luther, and indeed it is no more. God, in giving all the things of the world to Turks and wicked ones, His enemies, shows there is not much excellency and good in them. God, therefore, will cast them promiscuously up and down in the world because He looks upon them as worthless things. God does not so much regard whether men are prepared to give Him the glory of them or not; they shall have them however He is content to venture them. Indeed, when God comes unto His choice mercies in Christ, there He looks to have glory from them, and He never gives them to any but first He prepares them that they may give Him the glory of those mercies— but it is otherwise with others.

Suppose you see a man gathering apples, although swine are under the tree. He does not care much to drive them away. They are only apples; let the swine have them. But if he were gathering any choice and precious fruit, if any swine should come under, he would drive them away. As for outward things, apples, the Lord suffers the swine of the world to come grunting and take them up; but when He comes to His choice mercies in His Christ, there He makes a distinction. Oh, that is precious fruit! A blacksmith who is working upon iron, though a great many cinders and little bits of iron fly up and down, he does not regard them; but a goldsmith who is working upon gold preserves every ray and speck of dust of it. A jeweler who is working upon precious stones will be sure to preserve every little bit; a carpenter who is only hewing timber does not much mind if chips fly up and down, but it is not so with a jeweler. So these outward things are but as the chips and cinders, and such kind of things as those are, and therefore God even gives a portion to wicked men out of them.

6. God knows that He has time enough to manifest His justice upon them hereafter. He has eternity hereafter for the declaration of His justice, and therefore (says God), "Let them have something for a while."

As you know, it is natural in all, when they see a man going to execution who is not likely to live more than an hour or two, to pity him and be in any way officious to him. "Oh," we say, "the man shall not have comfort long! We cannot do much for him; he shall have pain enough ere long, and misery enough ere long." And so every one pities him. It is observable, let a man go to execution for wickedness and then he is pitied by all; but if a man should suffer for godliness, then, perhaps, they will not be so full of pity towards him.

As I remember in the *Book of Martyrs*, there is a story of Mr. John Frith (a learned, godly minister) and Andrew Hewit, who were martyrs, and were to suffer for their con- sciences. The story tells us that one Dr. Cook, a parson in London, openly admonished the people that they should pray for them no more than they would do for a dog; that charity of theirs that they talked so much of is such to- wards them who suffer out of conscience; and, as among papists, so among ungodly men. Let a man suffer out of conscience, and they will rather rail at him. When he is in his sufferings, they will rather give him gall and vinegar to drink, as they once did Christ upon the cross; though, in other sufferings, they pity men.

7. By this that God gives to the wicked, the Lord shows what great things He has reserved for His own children, what a portion there is for them. Surely, if the dogs have so much, the father keeps a good house; if the hanger-on may have such doles, certainly there is good provision for the children within. By the afflictions of the saints, God declares to wicked men and would have them draw such

an argument from it, that these are fearful things that are likely to befall them. "If judgment begins at the house of God, where shall the wicked and ungodly appear?" So by the prosperity that wicked men have in this world, God declares to His children, and He would have them argue from thence, what then has He reserved for His beloved ones, for His saints, for His children, who are so dear to Him?

8. God fetches a great deal of glory from hence. He fetches about His own ends very much from the portion that wicked men have. Sometimes He does it that they might stumble and harden their hearts, break their necks at it, and ripen their sins. Hence He lets them go on a long time and have their wills. Isaiah 33:1: "Woe to thee that spoilest, and thou wast not spoiled; and dealest treacherously with thee, and they dealt not treacherously with thee; when thou shalt cease to spoil, thou shalt be spoiled." In other words, "I'll let you go on. You shall spoil as much as you will, and, when you have done spoiling, you shall be spoiled."

Sometimes God does it to fetch about this end, namely, to chastise His own people with the prosperity of the wicked. An ancient writer has this story of one who (he says), by an extraordinary way, from being a monk was advanced into an episcopal seat and, being a lewd, wicked man, he began to be proud of his advancement; and, being proud, he heard these words: "Why are you so proud, O unhappy man, for you are not advanced because you are worthy of this advancement, but because this city is so ill." It is worthy of such a prelate to be over it in way of judgment to that place God advanced such a man. And so many are advanced that they may be heavy judgments unto others. God gives them such a portion not out of His love to them (though they are ready to gather the argument), but out of His displeasure unto others. And then He gives a plentiful portion to many to teach us all to do good unto our enemies; not only to human nature, but to men, to men who are wicked; some good must be done unto them.

9. The Lord would show hereby that He would have no argument of love or hatred to be drawn from these outward things, and also because He would not have them to expect any more. It may be that many men who are ungodly, prospering in this world, gather this argument that, therefore, God loves them and intends mercy to them. Nay, you may rather gather an argument quite the other way because God intends no further good unto you hereafter; therefore it is that you have so much now. We used to answer men who come for their dole, who have had out a dole, and they will come again. "Why do you come again? You have had your dole already." So God will answer to many men when they shall cry to Him for mercy at that day, "Why do you come to me for more? You have had your dole already; have you not had already more than your work comes to, more than you have done? You have had your part and portion already." Indeed, men speak much of God's mercy, and the mercy of God we acknowledge to be very great and glorious. Well, God shows Himself glorious in mercy that you, being so wicked, have as much as you have in this world; and, therefore, you should be denied eternal mercy hereafter. Yet you have cause to tell devils and damned creatures, who shall be your company, that God was very merciful to you while you lived in this world. You had something then, but here's all.

PARTICULAR 2. Here is all that you are likely to have:

1. Because there are some men whose names are written in the earth, and not in the Book of Life. In Jeremiah 17:13, it speaks of men who are written in the earth, whereas the saints are described to be men that are redeemed from the earth. In Revelation 14:3, it is their happiness to be redeemed from the earth; and it is all the

happiness you have, that you are written in the earth.

2. Here is their portion, because they are vile in the eyes of God. If you should ask the question, "Why do you give bones to the dog, and swill to the swine, and nothing else?" the answer would be, "Because it is a dog that has it, and because it is a swine; it is dog's meat." Certainly God speaks very contemptibly of all ungodly ones in the world, let them be never so great in regard of outward things. Daniel 11:21, "A vile person shall arise." Who is this vile person? Interpreters generally agree that it is Antiochus Epiphanes, who was a mighty great prince, such a prince as when the Samaritans wrote to him, they wrote "to Antiochus, the great god." His very name shows him to be a great one. Antiochus Epiphanes is as much as "Antiochus the Illustrious and the Famous." Yet, when the Holy Ghost speaks of him, it is "Antiochus, a vile person." They are vile in the eyes of God. If there are any in a family that you care not much for, you make no great provision for them. "Doth God take care for oxen?" They have something, but it is little. Does God take care for wicked and ungodly ones?

3. Here is their portion; it is confined to this life. Why so? Because they choose it themselves; and in that they have no wrong done to them. They make choice of this portion themselves. Moses, speaking to the people, said, "I set before you life and death." So do the ministers of God in preaching to you: they set before you life and death. What do you choose? Now, you choose the way that goes out of life and into death. You have but your choice; you choose vanity to be your portion. God does you no wrong to give you vanity. Now, you who will indent with God for your penny cannot take it ill if, when the end of the day comes, God puts you off with your penny. You know those in the vineyard who agreed for their penny began to murmur indeed when they came to receive their wages. "But," said the master of the vineyard, "did you not agree

with me so?" So you agree with God. All you intend in God's service is that you may have some present comfort in this world. You dare not trust God for the future; and here is that God will show His infinite displeasure against the sin of distrust by, that when the Lord propounds now, in this day of grace, such glorious and blessed things to the children of men, and (for all you know) any of you may have your portion in them as well as others, and yet you dare not trust God for those gracious things.

You think rather with yourselves, "Let me have something now, something for the present, some present pay." The reward that you talk of which is to come, I do not know whether they are imaginations or not. Therefore, you mean (it seems) to serve God for your present pay, and present pay you shall have and no more. There are some servants who are your day-servants; they serve you so that they expect their pay at night and, perhaps, you give them their two shillings at night and there is the end of it. But there are other servants now who will serve you in expectation of some reversions and expectations of honor, especially when they serve noblemen and princes. Though they have now present pay given to them at night, yet they go on cheerfully in their service. They expect some great reversions, like leases and preferments, afterwards. And now, though they did not get their two shillings a day as the others did, yet when the other befalls them they are made rich men, they and their posterities.

So, now, the poor man who has his pay every day, when a lease and preferment falls, if he should come in for his part he says, "Here was one who was content to rely and trust upon me and had no pay; and he trusted me, and now he comes to be preferred."

This is the direct difference between the men of the world and God's saints. The men of the world will do nothing without present pay; that which is just before them, they must have. Their hearts are upon it; but the saints hear what a blessed thing God has revealed in this Word, what a blessed covenant of grace there is, what rich promises of glorious things to come. Now they believe God and trust in God for these, and they say, "Lord, let me have my portion in the life to come, and whatever Thou dost with me here, I care not." It was the speech of Augustine, "Lord, here burn, here cut, but spare hereafter. I am content Lord, to be burnt, to be cut, to endure anything in the world, and sufferings in the world for Thee. Only hereafter I look for something else, and I'll wait for hereafter." You will not wait for hereafter, but you must have it for the present, and that is the reason you are put off here. Oh, it is a serious thing I speak of to you! Many a soul will wring its hands and curse itself eternally that it was not content to trust God for hereafter, but would have present pay.

You who are great merchants, if you buy a thing that is but a trifle, you pull out your purse and give the money down presently. But suppose you go to the exchange, and bargain for £10,000 there; you may give a little down now, but the great pay must come upon paydays afterwards. It is not expected that it should be presently done. So there are some men in the world who will trade with God, but they trade with God for peddling things, for their credit and applause, and for their preferments and estates. God gives the pay presently. You shall have it; there is your pay presently; it is done.

But now there are others of God's saints who trade with God for great things, for immortality and glory and a kingdom and a crown of eternal life. They expect not to have it done presently; they are content to stay. Oh, these are the best traders, the best merchants, who will trade with God for great things and be content to stay. You will choose what you have here for the present, and, therefore, you have your portion.

4. These things that are here are the only unsuitable

things to your hearts, and what will you do with any more hereafter? These things exceedingly please you and give you contentment as agreeable to you, and the things that are to come are disagreeable. What would men do who are carnal and wicked now? What would they do in heaven? Certainly, if you hate God's saints now (who have but a little grace) for their grace's sake, you would hate them infinitely more afterwards when they are perfect in grace, when they shall be perfect, and then when all your common gifts shall be taken away, for so it shall be. Now the things of God are unsuitable to you, though you have now many common gifts; and you now abhor the grace of God, though it is imperfect. What, then, when all common gifts shall be taken from you and grace made perfect? How unsuitable will it be then to you? Therefore, expect nothing hereafter.

5. You abuse your portion you have now; what will you do with more? Who will trust you with the true riches? You abuse what you have. Indeed, men of the world who are wicked and very rich are presently in places of honor and power. Oh! what a deal of mischief they do in the world! What dreadful evils are they unto the earth! Such men, how they abuse their portions! Why now, as it is with the tooth in a man's head; a tooth indeed is preferred to have an eminent place in the head, but when the tooth comes to be rotten and puts us to pain, what do we but pull it out and throw it away? So when God prefers men to eminent places, when through their wickedness they grow rotten, and so do a great deal of hurt, the Lord plucks them out in His anger and throws them away. They abuse their portion and do a great deal of hurt, and, therefore, must expect no more.

6. But above all, the argument is that they have no interest in Jesus Christ. The rich treasures of the infinite grace of God are let out in Jesus Christ. God has divers conduit pipes (if I may so say) of His grace to let out unto

His creatures. There are some lesser conduit pipes, and those conduit pipes may be opened through the general bounty of God; but now the Lord has the great current of His eternal mercies for some to whom He intends eternal good, and this great current of His is stopped by justice. The infinite justice of God stops this great current so that it cannot be opened to have any drop of the mercy let out until divine justice comes to be satisfied. In the meantime, through the other smaller pipes runs the general bounty of God.

Now, then, this is the very work of Jesus Christ, Christ the second Person in the Trinity, and it is the very mystery of the gospel. The second Person in the Trinity sees that the children of men are capable of eternal happiness, eternal glory, and that there are glorious treasures with God to be communicated to the children of men; but through man's sin this great current is stopped. In the meantime, God's general bounty lets out a great many outward comforts. Christ, therefore, out of pity to mankind, that mankind may not be put off with these general outward comforts, comes and satisfies God's infinite justice so that He might open the current, the sluice of God's infinite grace and mercy to them. As for the men of the world, they have but a little of the drizzlings of God's general bounty through some crannies, but the floodgates of God's grace are opened in Christ. Therefore, till divine justice is satisfied, there can be no further good for a creature here but the fruits of God's general bounty and patience.

There are some creatures whom the Lord has left to the course of justice. They shall have what they earn and no more. This is the difference between God's dealings with some creatures and others. I say, there are some who shall have what they earn and no more; others there are whom God has set His heart upon, and, whether they earn or not, God intends eternal mercies unto them and will bring them unto eternal mercies. Here's the difference between the covenant of works and the covenant of grace; and, therefore, the one is left to himself, and the other, Christ the Head of the covenant, comes to undertake for him what he cannot do. And here is the very cut between the condition of some men and other men, who some have their portion in this world and others have another higher portion in the world to come. Those have no interest in Christ; these do.

7. They are no sons, no children, and therefore they must not expect children's portions. Many of you rich men, when you die, will leave your servants some legacy. Perhaps you'll give every servant in the house five pounds or so; but when you come to your children, to write in your will what such a son, such a daughter shall have, that is another manner of business: you'll leave them forty or fifty great things.

Now, the truth is, the world may be divided between children and servants; for though the truth is that all men are defiant with God, yet God makes them servants one way or other; and there is some little legacy that servants shall have, but they must not expect the children's portion. Therefore, they have it here, but must not have it hereafter. Ezekiel 46:16–17: "Thus saith the Lord God, 'If the Prince give a gift unto any of his sons, the inheritance thereof shall be his son's; but if to his servants, then it shall be his to the year of liberty.' " It was God's law that if a prince gave a gift to his son, the son would inherit it forever, but if he gave it but to a servant, it would continue with him but for a while. So here is the difference between God's administration of all His gifts: He gives some to servants, and these shall continue but for a while; within a little while all will be called for again. All the good, and all the comfort you have, God will call for it all again; but that which He gives to his sons, to His children, they shall have mercy forever, though not enjoy it in the same way. They shall enjoy the same good and comfort eternally.

8. The portion that the world has (you heard before) comes from God's patience; but there will be an end of the manifestation of the glory of patience in this world. As there are some graces of the Spirit of God in the saints that shall have an end, in regard of their exercise here in this world, so there are some attributes of God that shall have an end in regard of the manifestation of them in the way that God now manifests them here in this world, that is, the patience of God towards ungodly ones. Now, if they hold all upon patience, when the time of the glory of that in this world shall come to be at an end, then all their good is at an end.

9. Ungodly men shall have to deal with God immediately in the world to come. They must have to deal immediately with God in the world to come. Now they have to deal with God through creatures and, while they have to deal with God through creatures, they may get a great deal, and may make shift for much; but when they shall come to deal with God immediately, then it will be other ways with them. For example, there are a great many hangers-on at great men's houses; and, perhaps, when they have to deal with the servants, they get some bits and scraps and many things from the servants; but, if they know they can have nothing but from the very hand of the knight, of the lord of the house himself, then they will expect no great matter.

So, the wicked men of this world are as hangers-on: all that they have are but as scraps from the servants. They have to deal only with creatures; they look no further. But hereafter things shall be settled another way, and all things shall be weighed by God Himself in a balance of justice, and distributed by the hands of God Himself immediately. And now things will be carried after another manner; the Lord Himself will come to dispose of things.

It was a speech of a German divine that, though he was

a good man and lived very innocently, when he lay upon his sick bed and apprehended death, he was in great terrors of spirit, mightily troubled. Some of his friends came to him and asked, "Why would you be so troubled, who has lived so good a life as you have done?"

This was his answer: "The judgments of God are one thing and the judgments of men are another. I am now to deal with God. It is true, I lived thus before men, and men gave their verdict of me as good, and thought I was in a good condition. But, oh, I am now to go to God and deal immediately with Him, and God's judgment, and man's judgments are different things!"

When God shall come to weigh all men's portions out, as it will be then, so much righteousness, so much portion, so much happiness, you'll say then, "Lord, what shall become of us all? All our righteousness is as the menstruous cloth." Aye, but for the saints, the righteousness of Christ will be put into one scale and their portion into the other, and their portion will be weighted by the righteousness of Christ. Now, when you come to God, you must come to the scale, and you will put in your good serving of God, your coming to church, some good civil actions, and natural and moral things you have done. You will put them in the scale. God says, "That which you have had already weighs down all those; have you nothing to put into the scales but this? You have had your reward already for all this, and much more than this. Then, if there is nothing to put into the scale but this, you are undone, and there is nothing for you for eternity." And here is the ground of the confinement of the portions of wicked men. These are the two first things.

PARTICULAR 3. I will give you some corollaries from what has been said. Is it so that wicked men have a portion here, and here is all?

COROLLARY 1. Here we may see the reason why the men of the world are so cunning in the things of the world, why they can make so good a shift for themselves in the world rather than other men can. Why? Here is their portion; their very happiness and good is here. No marvel that they make such shift as they do here. The apostle said in 1 Corinthians 2:12, "We have received not the spirit of the world." We cannot tell how to shift in the world as other men do, for, indeed, we look further than these things and so cannot shift as other men can. They who have the spirit of the world, and have their portion in the world, can shift; but we have not received the spirit of the world.

You know a swine, though it goes abroad all day wandering up and down, knows the way to the trough at night; but if a sheep goes wandering a little way out of his place, it does not know how to come back again, but wanders up and down till it is lost. It is a lost sheep when it is wandering up and down; but swine are not so. So ungodly men, though they go wandering up and down, know how to come to their trough at night. They have better skills in the world; they are more artificial in the things of the world; they have better understanding (as the Scripture speaks): "The children of this world are wiser in their generation, than the children of light." Why is it? Their portion is in this world.

COROLLARY 2. Here we see the reason why there are so many great ones in the world who regard religion as little as they do, and the ways of God and the church of God. Why? It is not their portion. Those things that concern another life are not any part of their portion. They mind what it is that concerns the present life because that is their portion. When many come into places of dignity and power, what are their thoughts? Why, now they think of gratifying their friends; they think of respect and honor that they shall have abroad in the world, and be accounted somebody; they think of revenging all their wrongs, of making up of all their broken titles. This has been, heretofore (I suppose very ordinarily), in men advanced among you; these are all their thoughts. As for doing service for God and the church, and indicating the truth and honor of God, that is scarcely in any of their thoughts, for they do not look upon that as part of their portion.

Here is the reason why so many magistrates are like Gallio in Acts 18:17: "Gallio cared for none of those things." They were to him but matters of words, and yet they were about the great fundamental points of religion: whether Christ was the true Messiah, whether He was God or not. But to Gallio, these things were but matter of words. And so the great things of God and religion, to carnal hearts, are things that are of no great consequence at all. Yea, when Sosthenes, who was the ruler of the synagogue for countenancing Paul, had the rude multitude of the city rise up in a rude manner to apprehend him and lay violent hands upon him, Gallio cared for none of these things; but so far he did not go. Gallio went not to stir up a rude multitude to lay violent hands upon a ruler of a synagogue or a city, but he cared for none of those things, the text says. What did he care for those things, the text asks. What did he care for rectifying anything that was amiss in religion? "Oh, let us (say those who have their portion here), whatever becomes of things, let us make peace that we may go on and be quiet in our houses, and enjoy what we have quietly and peaceably." And they look no further: Why? Their portion is here, and as for truth, how they reject and condemn it!

It is a speech (as is credibly reported) that has come even from a citizen here in cursing the truth (as, had he lived among the Jews, he would certainly have been stoned to death), "Let us have peace and a pox of truth." I say, such a speech as this among the Jews would have caused him to have been stoned to death, being such horrible blasphemy.

But how many are ready to say with Pilate, in John 18:38, when Christ was before Pilate and talked to him of truth: "Truth?" said Pilate, "what is truth?" It is as if Pilate had said, "What a strange man is this? The man is in danger of his life and he talks of truth when he is in danger of his life! What is truth?" And Pilate turned it back upon Him presently.

Just so are the hearts of many. What? Should we look at truth, or at anything now but to preserve our lives, estates, and outward comforts in the world? What is truth? They are a company of mad-brained fellows who are factious and seditious; they talk of truth and know not what they say. "Come, let us have peace, though it be upon any terms." Who is there in this place that does not desire peace? The Lord knows it is the desires of those who are accused most for want of desires in this thing; yea, so we dare challenge any of you with this challenge. Those who have been most at the throne of grace, begging God for peace for England, let them carry the day; those who have put forth most prayers for peace before the throne of grace, we are willing they shall have the day. We read that, among all the tribes that came up in a war-like way to help the people of God against oppression, in Judges 5:18, and so in the chapter, that of all, Naphtali was the only tribe that joined with Zebulun, who jeopardized their lives in the cause of God, who would take up arms to defend themselves and the people against oppression.

Surely these two tribes, by the others that would take up arms to defend themselves and the people against oppression; surely these two tribes, by the others that would not venture themselves, were at that time accounted very factious and very seditious. What? They? Only Zebulun and Naphtali? Yet it is observable that, though there were none joined with Zebulun but Naphtali, there is no tribe of which it is so much spoken to be a tribe full of courtesy and civility, of a peaceable and quiet disposition, as

Naphtali was. You shall find, if you read Genesis 49:21, there are these two things said of Naphtali: he was as a hind let loose, and he gave goodly words. But they may be but words of complement, not reality. Nay (when Moses comes with the blessing, you shall find these two places, one in Genesis, and the other in Deuteronomy), when Moses comes with the blessing again upon Naphtali: "Naphtali was filled with favor, and with the blessing of the Lord." What is the meaning? Naphtali was a tribe that had the most courtesy and civility of all; one that gave courteous language to all, and not mere words, but reality. It was such a one that was filled with favor, that had the favor of God and the favor of men. He had such a courteous carriage, and he had the blessing of God upon him; and yet this Naphtali was the tribe that would jeopardize their lives and take up arms in defense of the people of God against oppression in those times above all. And Phinehas, you know, was so zealous and would make use of the sword so as he did; yet in Numbers 25:12-13 God said that He would make a covenant of peace with him. Beloved! Phinehas is such a fiery hot man, yet a covenant of peace must be made with him by God Himself; for he did indeed, by that way, procure peace to Israel. The text says there in Numbers that because Phinehas "was so zealous," it was, "that I consumed not the children of Israel."

Now, it's observable, the word in the original is "because he was zealous, therefore it was that I might not consume them in My zeal." It's translated in your books, "because he was thus zealous, that I might not consume them in My jealousy." The words are different in the English, but in the Hebrew they are the same, and so are turned thus: "because he was so zealous, it was that I might not consume them in My zeal." It is as if he should have said, "If there had not been some among them who had been zealous (and, as they account, fiery), I would have been zealous Myself, and fiery Myself, and consumed them." It was well they had such among them, and one day those who cry out of them may come to see cause to bless God for them who would not have the world put off, and gulled with the fair name of peace.

We know the devil has made much use of it in former times, and would fain make use of it now, as if those who desired truth most were not greatest friends unto peace. God forbid that it should be so; though it is true, we do not think we have our portion here; and, therefore, we would not have peace upon any terms. Indeed we confess our portion lies higher, and that wherein our portion consists we would have upon any terms. Therefore Paul said in Philippians 3:11: "If by any means, I might attain unto the resurrection of the dead." As if he were saying, "If by any means, upon any terms, that I may have peace at the great day, whatsoever I do endure." So say we for our portion.

Yet you say, "Let us have peace upon any terms." Why? Because your portion is here. We would be glad that all our mountains were mountains of Olivet, but we would be loath to have the mountains of corruption. In 2 Kings 23:13, you read of a "mount of corruption," of offense—so it is in the old Latin. Now, what was that same mountain of corruption? If we compare one Scripture with another, we shall find it was no other than Mount Olivet. Mount Olivet was made a mountain of corruption. In 1 Kings 11:7, Solomon built idolatrous temples for the honor of the gods that his queen worshipped. Solomon built temples to gratify her, and it was upon the mount before Jerusalem, which was the Mount of Olivet. Now you know that Mount Olivet was a mount that had its name from olives that grew there, and were emblems of peace; yet the Mount of Olives may be made a mount of corruption. We would be glad that we might live upon Mount Olivet all our days, but are loath this Mount Olivet should be made a mount of corruption. Give me leave but in a few words yet to put some considerations to you, and, if I speak not reason in them, reject them.

First, because you are so greedy of comforts in this world, you would fain have peace, and be wise even for your own portion. You would have peace, but, I hope, a safe peace, and that is all you desire. If the peace is not safe, oh, the blood that may follow after! We read in Acts 27:13 that there was indeed a calm ("and the south wind blew softly for a while"), warm wind. Not long after, it appears that "there arose a tempestuous wind called Euroclydon." Take heed, my brethren, that we are not deluded with the soft south wind; take heed that there is not a Euroclydon that blows presently after. Were we sure to be delivered from that same Euroclydon, we should be glad of continuance of soft blowings of the south wind. Can you think of a safe peace that lives under any arbitrary governments? "No," you'll say, "and therefore we account our condition ill now, for we have arbitrary governments among us. And who are they?"

OBJECTION. Does not the Parliament govern in that kind of way?

ANSWER. Give me leave in a word to answer this. Consider the difference between that arbitrary government the Parliament complains of and what now you feel.

ANSWER 1. That was then, when the kingdom was in a settled way, and then when there was no contrary arbitrary power to oppose it, yet then it went on. And surely, then, it only made way for a worse arbitrary government; but now it is in a way when the kingdom is unsettled, and in a way where there is a necessity of some help beyond the ordinary course of law because of a contrary, arbitrary power that is opposed. And is it possible for any man who has any wisdom or understanding in his head to not see the difference between these two? But I'll show you a greater difference than this.

ANSWER 2. That was before those who so governed

suffered nothing in it themselves, but gained all. Now those who are accused for the present, if it is arbitrary, suffer themselves as much as we do, and their posterity suffers as much as we do. And therefore, the thing is far different from what was before. And yet, further, if you would not be carried away with words, but judge righteous judgment, consider this:

ANSWER 3. Can you think that if the adversaries should prevail, you would be only at the disposal of the King? Do you not think that those who are with him, and give such strength and assistance for the present, that you must lie at their mercy too, in great part? And will that be safe for you? I put it to every man's conscience whether he can think that it is safer for church or commonwealth to be governed by the King, with those who are now about him, and as an army of papists, than to be governed by the King, with his two Houses of Parliament? Which is the safest way in the consciences of any man living? And yet further than this, consider (if you have your eyes in your heads).

ANSWER 4. Perhaps what you aim at as your end, your adversaries may aim at as their means, and what will become of you then? If what you would have as an end they shall look at as a means, consider what consequences may come of it.

ANSWER 5. You who desire so much peace to preserve your own portions here, would you not willingly have such peace as those who have appeared for you in Houses of Parliament in the city, in the ministry, who have been most active, be preserved too? Are you so desirous of it as to be willing to leave them to the fury and rage of their adversaries? Would not this be one of the most horrible wickednesses that ever was committed in a kingdom, if they, from desire to save their own states particularly, should betray those who have been faithful to them in their places of trust? Once Demosthenes, in a speech to one who would fain have peace, affirmed that it is vain and a preposterous thing to desire peace with the flock upon this condition: "that the keeper of the flock may but be betrayed, and taken away." The fair name of peace will never so prevail with a wise man when he shall come to be the condition of it. The good people in Chrysostom's time (however you may think of those who have most appeared for you, and ventured themselves) thought it such a thing to have but the mouth of one Chrysostom stopped that they professed.

If the sun should take back, or bring back, and keep in arrays, it would be more tolerable then than that the mouth of John should be stopped—they had such a high esteem of a faithful minister in those times. Therefore, if you would be faithful to God, to the kingdom, and to those who have appeared for you, look after such peace as wherein you and they may be safe. God knows they would have been willing to have been as silent as you; but suppose all the ministers of the kingdom, and men who had ability to appear publicly, had all been silent, so as the business had been wholly betrayed, and at length an army of papists had risen when you had had no help to resist them. Would you not have cried out of ministers? Would you not have cried out of magistrates? Would you not have cried out of Parliament men? If they have ventured themselves to be faithful for you, know you can have no peace unless they have it; and it were an unworthy thing, to think of your safety without theirs likewise.

OBJECTION. But you will say, "We would not have our estates and peace thus as you speak, upon any terms, without any regard to religion. We have our portion in religion as well as you, and we have our consciences to look after well as you. God forbid it should be otherwise but that religion should prosper too without peace; but we would not have such sects and sectaries to be maintained in the kingdom. Let us have truth and religion, but away with them.

ANSWER 1. Do you understand what you speak of? Do you know wherein you and they differ? You cry out of them as if they were of another religion, whereas, when it comes to be scanned, the difference between you and them will not be so great. But, further, I put this to you:

ANSWER 2. Do you spend as much breath in praying for these kinds of men as you do in railing upon them? Then something may be said.

ANSWER 3. It is a vain thing to think that true religion can be maintained, and have the liberty of it, without some difference of opinion among us. Indeed, the Turks have as much peace in their religion as any religion has in all the world. And there is as little difference of opinion among the Turks as there is in any religion whatsoever; but well may that coat have no seam that has no shape. If the truth of religion comes to appear, certainly it is impossible but many differences of opinion must come. It is a most intolerable pride of heart, and tyranny in any whatsoever, to think by violent means to force all to be of the same opinion that they are of in matters that are not foundational, and that may stand with the peace of a commonwealth too. You take upon you in that, more than Christ does, more than the apostles ever did.

OBJECTION. But, you will say, "If men are in error, why should they not be forced? Shall every man be left to his opinion, to do what he will?"

ANSWER. No, I plead not for that either. Therefore I except all opinions, first, against the foundation of religion, and, second, all those opinions that are against the foundation of civil government. Take those two aside, and then, for other opinions that are of a lower, inferior nature (I say), there you take too much upon you, whoever you are, if you should think to force men to be of the same opinion as you are. And there is no such way to make disturbance in churches and commonwealth as to force men to be of the same opinion in things that are of an inferior nature.

OBJECTION. Aye, but you'd still say, "If it is an error, they must not be left to live in it!"

ANSWER. Nay, stop there, A man may be in an error, and yet you have nothing to do to offer violence unto him, to bring him out of his error. You may seek to convince him as much as you can, but to offer violence you undertake more than God has given you commission to do, whatever you are. I give this clear Scripture for it in Romans 14.2: "One believeth that he may eat all things, another who is weak eateth herbs. Let not him that eateth despise him that eateth not, and let not him which eateth not judge him that eateth." And so he tells us, "Who art thou that judgest another? Who art thou that judgest?" These two opinions could not be true: one man eats herbs; the other man makes conscience of it and cannot do it. Certainly one of these was a sin at that time. One of them was a sin, to eat herbs, and that he might eat no flesh, for God never commanded them that they should eat no flesh; to make conscience to eat no flesh was a sin, yet though one were a sin, they who were in the right must not by violence force those who were in the wrong to their opinion, but they must leave them to God. I say, in matters of such consequence as these, it is a point of antichristian tyranny and pride, and notorious pride in men who have taken so much upon them as to force all to be of the same opinion. Certainly, this is not the way for true peace.

COROLLARY 3. If men have their portion in this world, here is the reason: There is such a stir in the world by men to maintain their portion. What a deal of stir is there! What rending and tearing is there that they might maintain their estates! Especially if some men have a higher portion in the world than others, oh, what a deal of stir is there to maintain it! I remember Henry IV wrote to Pope Gregory and told him that, by reason of an

Emulation there was about the Pope-dom, one being chosen in Rome and the other in another place, that 230,000 men lost their lives out of that Emulation. Two men, two Popes, cost the blood of 230,000 men. Oh, what a stir is there in the world to satisfy the wills of a few men in the world!

Certainly one day the world will be wiser, and will understand that they are men and not dogs, that they were not made to be subject to the humors and the lusts of men, and that no man has now any further power over him but that they have by agreement from them, one way or other, either implicit or explicit, one way or other; it is by their agreement, that any man has any power over them, and can exercise any. The world ere long, I hope, will be wise enough to understand this, and therefore will not so sacrifice their lives for the satisfying of the wills of a few men in the world. They shall not make such a stir in the world as heretofore they have done. Indeed, men make a great stir now to maintain their portions, for the contention is not about matters of bounds and limits, but it is about the inheritance itself; it is about their portion: It is their god. "And do you say, 'What ails me?' when you have taken away my gods?" Here is the ground of all the stirs and combustions in the world: Carnal hearts look upon what they enjoy as their portion. But how comes it to pass that men should be so greedy of their portion? Is it such an excellent portion that they are so greedy of it? Is it worth so much that they contend so much about it? This makes way for me to slip into the fourth particular.

PARTICULAR 4. What kind of portion is this that these men of the world have that they make such a stir about? To make way for that:

One, consider what poor things they are that they make such a stir about.

Second, consider the tenure upon which they hold whatever they enjoy.

Third, consider the mixture of evil that there is in what they enjoy.

Fourth, consider the blessed portion that they lose that they might enjoy.

Last, consider the dreadful end that there will be to such men who have their portion here.

1. What are the poor things that men have here in this world? Their comforts, for the most part, are but imaginary; Hosea 12:1: "Ephraim feedeth on wind." When a bladder is full of wind, one prick lets it all out; so when death comes, it lets out all their comforts. Even as the wind goes all out at one prick in a bladder, so all the comforts of the men of the world go out by the prick of death. Proverbs 23:5: "Wilt thou set thine eyes upon that which is not?" It is not; it has no reality in it. In Acts 25, when Bernice and Agrippa came in great pomp and state to the assembly, that which you have in your books translated "great pomp" is, in the Greek, "with great fancy." All the pomp and jollity in the world is but a fancy; this is their portion.

That which they have is of a very low nature; this would be an argument over which we might philosophize if it were fit or we had time, but I'll quickly pass over these things. It's of a very low nature; it not much concerns the soul, all the portion they have. Therefore, says the text, "Thou fillest their belly." It is but a belly full, and what is that to the soul? Indeed, the rich man in the gospel could say, "Soul, take thy ease, for thou hast goods laid up for many years, eat, drink." Will you say, "Soul, take thy ease, because thou hast goods laid up, and because you may eat, and drink?" What is all this to the soul? Ambrose had such a speech upon the place, "If the man had the soul of a swine, what could be said otherwise?" For, indeed, these things were suitable to the soul of a swine. You shall find that a man is not the better because of outward things, not a whit.

The heart of the wicked is of little worth; his estate may be worth something; his house may be worth something; his lands may be worth something, but "the heart of the wicked is little worth" (Proverbs 10:20). And would not you think it a great evil if, when you go up and down abroad, you should know for certain that no man gives you any respect but for the sake of your servant who attends you? Would not that discourage and trouble you? Indeed, you come to such a man's house, and he seems to make you welcome and entertains you. Aye, but you come to know afterwards that it was not for your sake, but for your servant's sake that he loved you. Would you think you had a good entertainment there? The truth is, all the respect you have in this world is for your servant's sake, for your goods, house, and lands; it is not for any worth that is in you. Socrates spoke once to one Achilous, when he had a fine house and many brave things there, "There are many who come to see your house and your fine furniture, but they see no worth in you." Indeed, all these things are not foul's meat. It is not man's meat they feed upon; it is but ashes; it is nothing to the soul of man.

Suppose it were for the soul. What you have here is but a very poor pittance, a scanty portion. You do not have all the world; you have your portion in this world. If you have the whole world at commands, yea, if God should make a thousand worlds more for you to command, this would be all but a poor pittance with which to put off an immortal soul. But now what you have is but a little minim in the world. All nations of the earth are but as the dust of the balance, and a drop in the bucket to God. What is your dust then? What is your house and land then? Socrates wittily rebuked the pride of Alcibiades, when he was very proud that he had so much land laying together. He brought his map of the world to him, and said, "Pray show me where your land lies here." One prick of a pen would have described it all. Should we take a rich man here who had a great deal of land, and bring a map of the world to him, England, Ireland, and Scotland are but three little spots to the world. And what are your farms and the manors you have? You have but a little portion, and if you had all it would be no great matter. The truth is, all you have in this world cannot be enough to make you live in fashion in the world like a man. It's not enough (I say) to live like a man in the world, to live like one who has an immortal soul, like one who has the image of God upon him, and was sent hither into the world to do some great service as every one of you was sent here to do. Therefore it is but a mean thing; little cause you have for to rejoice in it.

It's true, those who are godly account themselves unworthy of the least thing they have here in the world, but I'll tell you a mystery of religion now, a practical maxim of religion, that is a great mystery to the world: a gracious heart, though he thinks himself unworthy of the least crumb of bread, yet all the creatures in heaven and earth will not serve to be his portion. He is satisfied with anything, counting himself unworthy of the meanest condition in this world as a present gift of God; but if God should give him heaven and earth, he would not be satisfied unless God gives him Himself. Therefore, certainly your portion is but a very small portion.

Those things that you have are things that will vanish and quickly come to nothing. It is said of the whole world, in Job 26:7 that whole earth hangs upon nothing. And so do all the things of the earth; and therefore it is said of Abraham in Hebrews 11 that he sought a city that had foundations. All other things are as things that have no foundation at all. There is a worm in every creature that will consume it in time; and the Scripture calls all our riches "uncertain riches." Christian, you are made for an eternal condition; these things are fading. When you come to enter into your eternal estate, if you should then ask, "What shall I have now? I have now this much and this much in my whole life; but what shall I have now? I come to enter into my eternal estate, and truly I have nothing at all."

If a man were to go on a great voyage to the Indies, and all the provision he makes is to get a vessel that can make shift to carry him as far as Gravesend; if he begins his voyage to the Indies, gets to the ocean, and finds, alas, that the vessel is a rotten vessel, would not this be an unwise man? Truly, this is the condition of thousands in the world. Man or woman, you are made for an eternal condition. God intends eternity to every mother's child that is here this day, and God expects that your life should be spent in making provision for this eternal estate of yours. Yet you think of nothing but that you may provide for a few years here, live in some fashion, and be somebody in this world. Oh, when you come to enter upon the ocean of eternity, you will give a dreadful shriek and cry out, "I am undone. I am undone. I have provided nothing for eternal life!" These things are very uncertain. Oh, what a deal of difference there is between the same men in two or three years! I might tell you (but the time so hastens) that great difference two or three years have made between man and men, but I forbear it because I see the time will not give leave.

Whatever you have in this world, it is no other but what may stand with the eternal hatred of an infinite God towards you. It may be the portion of a reprobate, and will this serve your turn? Will this satisfy you? Will that satisfy your soul that may be the portion of a reprobate? There are many now who are sweltering under the wrath of the infinite God, who have had 20 times as much as any of you have who are here before the Lord this day. They have had greater estates than you, lived merrier lives than you, and yet are now under the wrath of God. Will a reprobate's portion serve your turn? Therefore, surely, it is but a mean thing that will stand with God's eternal hatred.

Consider it, to enjoy the dominion of all the world may stand with God's eternal hatred, but to have but the least dram of saving grace cannot stand with God's eternal hatred. What a difference is there between the having the least dram of grace and the enjoyment of all the world? What a goodly portion is there here that you so much rejoice in? It is certainly because your heart is so straight that you think these things to be so big. In a narrow vessel a thing will appear big, but in a mighty, wide vessel it appears little. So when the Lord by grace shall widen and enlarge your heart, then all the things of the world will be little to you.

Grace has the image of God in it. Now what does God say of Himself in Isaiah 40 but that all the world is but as the drop of the bucket and the dust of the balance. Now grace has God's likeness, and through the image of God in a gracious heart the soul says of the world, as God said, "All the world is but as the drop of the bucket, and the dust of the balance to me." When the Lord promised to persuade Japhet, to dwell in the tents of Shem, the word that is translated "persuade" signifies "to enlarge," that He would enlarge the heart of Japhet. Indeed, when God converts a soul, He enlarges that soul, enlarges the heart, and therefore all the things of the world are now but little. Indeed, if a man is below here, and looks upon what is next to him that has any bigness in it, it looks like something great; but if a man were advanced on high, upon the top of a pinnacle, then what seemed great appears but little to him. So it is with the men of the world who here lie groveling below. The curse of the serpent is upon them: "Upon thy belly shalt thou go, and dust shalt thou eat." They think that things of the world are great matters; but grace lifts up the heart on high to God and Christ, mounts it up to eternity, and then they can look upon all these things here below as mean things.

This was the reason that Luther, when he had great gifts sent in to him by many of the great men of Saxony, began to be afraid lest the Lord should reject him here in this world. He had this expression, "I vehemently protested that God should not put me off so." That is his word, according to the manner of the man. According to the manner of his language thus he speaks. When there came in things of the world, and he began to be tickled with honor, and great men respected him, "Oh," he thought, "I shall be somebody now in the world!" Thus corruption began to work, but grace prevailed, and he broke out with this expression, "I protested that God should not put me off so. There are other things I look for, things that are better and higher; these are poor pittances for this soul of mine to be put off. There are other things I must have from the Lord or else I cannot be satisfied." That is the first thing, the poor things of the world, which are the portion of wicked men;

2. Consider the tenure by which they hold it. All you have in the world, you hold it not by a good tenure. It is not held *in capite;* that is not the tenure you hold it by. I confess this, I think not the men of the world to be usurpers for what they lawfully get in the world. I think not they shall answer merely for their using what they do, merely for their right to use what they have, but they shall answer for their not using it right. They shall not answer (I say) for their right to use, but for their not using it right. They have some right, but what right is it they hold it upon, what tenure? There is a three-fold right:

There is a right from justice that we may claim a thing by. One can claim by justice such a thing is his due; what is not your right, you cannot claim.

There is a right from creation that God gave to man at first creation; you have lost that too.

There is a right from promise. God has promised all good things to His people. You have not that right either;

you have neither the right from justice to claim, nor the right from creation, nor the right from promise. What right do you have then? There is a fourth right, and that right I confess you have:

There is a right from donation. God is pleased to give to you, but just this. You hold all your honors and estates, and you who are ungodly men are just as a man who is condemned to die. And there being a little reprieve for two or three days before his execution, the prince, out of his indulgence, gives order to have provision made for him according to his quality; that if he is a gentleman, he shall have such and such provision, if a knight, a nobleman, a peer of the realm, he shall have provision according to his quality until his execution. Now no man can say this man usurps, though he has forfeited all his right to his land and estate, yea if the king gives him this refreshment he is no usurper, but it is a poor right he has. It's a right from donation, and this God gives the ungodly men in this world. They have a right to outward comforts. You have your portion, but you see how you hold it.

That's the second thing. I have but one or two things more to dispatch of this particular, and then two things further and I shall wind up all as briefly as I can. I am told I may take some liberty at such a time as this, and seeing it is only the preaching opportunity we meddle with, give me leave a little the more to transgress upon your patience; in that, I hope, I shall not transgress very much.

3. The next thing to be considered is that this portion here, as it is poor in regard of the mean things and the tenure, so there is a great deal of mixture here in what you have.

(1) There is a manifold mixture of burden, of trouble, and the truth is that all the good things wicked men enjoy in this world will scarcely bear charges; that is, there is so much trouble they meet with here in this world with their portion that all they have will scarcely bear

charges. And if a man goes on a voyage, we used not to count anything he spends by the way to be part of his treasury. All we have here in this world is but spending money to bear our charges, in regard God knows we shall be at a great deal of charges, and afflictions we shall meet with here. But besides:

(2) There is a mixture of curse in every portion of an ungodly man. If any of you think you get such a rich match—you get a wife that is a very rich match, and you get her portion—and there you go and fetch away the bags of gold that are her portion; but if it should prove that every bag of gold you have of your wife's portion had the plague in it, it would be but a poor portion. Certainly it is thus with all ungodly ones in the world, that all the while they live, whatever they enjoy, as long as continuing wicked, they have a curse of God that goes along with it, and makes way unto eternal misery for them. As those who are godly have the blessing of God in outward things that makes way for their eternal good, so you have the curse of the Lord mingled with all your outward things that makes way for eternal evil unto you.

4. Consider what portion you lose. You have gotten one, but you lose a great deal more. If a man had been at the Exchange and made a bargain about some petty thing, and afterwards, when he came home, he knew that by not buying such a thing, he has lost a bargain that would have made him and his posterity, he has little cause of rejoicing in that bargain he has made. So, though you have gotten a portion that may seem to satisfy you somewhat, know you have lost a portion of infinite worth and value. It's impossible to show you what this portion is, for the devil could show Christ all the glory of the world in the twinkling of an eye; but if I should come to show you the glory of heaven, I would need to have eternity to show you what the portion of the saints is, but though I cannot show it all to you, I will only give you a hint or two that you may know

something of what it is:

(1) It is such a portion as is fit for the spouse of the Lamb, as is fit for the spouse of one who is to marry the Son of God, the second Person in the Trinity.

(2) It is such a portion as is fit and suitable to an heir of life and glory, an heir of heaven and earth.

(3) It is such a portion as God gives unto them to this very end, as to declare what the infinite power of God is able to do to raise a poor creature to the height of happiness. What do you think this must be? I say, it must therefore be done that it might declare to angels, and all creatures, what the infinite power of God is able to do to raise a poor creature to happiness and glory. This must be something.

(4) It must be such a one in which God must attain unto the great design that He had from all eternity in making the heavens and the earth. The special design that God had in making heaven and earth from all eternity was to magnify the riches of His grace to a company that He had set apart to glory. It must be such a portion, and guess what this must be.

(5) It is such a portion as must require the infinite power of God to support a creature so as to be able to bear the weight of that glory. It's such a portion. And do but think what kind of portion that must be?

6) All this must be now to all eternity. I remember that when Esau heard Isaac, his father, tell what a blessing he had given unto Jacob, the text says that Esau "fell a weeping." Oh, that God would strike upon the hearts of men who have so little minded anything but the present things of the world! You hear but a few words of what the Lord has reserved to all eternity for His saints, and compare that with what is your portion, and what is likely to be your portion, and you have cause to weep. Aye, but more cause you will have to weep if so be you consider the last thing.

5. Consider what is likely to be your end, your portion is in this world. If indeed you could, in this world, enjoy your heart's desire, and let that be your end, it would be something. Oh, but there is something else that remains afterwards:

(1) Oh, the perplexity of spirit that any worldly man will have when death comes, when he shall see an end of all the comforts of this world. Then it is "Farewell house, lands, friends, acquaintances, and all merry meetings and jovialities. I shall never have comfort more in you." It was the speech of Pope Adrian when he was to die: "Oh, my soul, my soul! Where are you going? Where are you going? You shall never have more jests, nor be merry, nor be jocund any more. Where are you going?" So may a man who has his portion in this world here say at his death, "Where is this poor soul of mine going? I have lived here this many years, and I have had many merry meetings. I have eaten of the fattest and drunk of the sweetest, and gone in brave array; but now my day is gone. What shall become of me? What peace have I now when all is gone?"

I remember [Hugh] Latimer had such a story in one of the sermons that he preached before King Edward. He tells a story of a rich man who, when he lay upon his sick bed, there came one who told him that certainly, by all reasons by which they can judge, he was likely to be a man for another world, a dead man. As soon as he heard these words (They are Latimer's words. I only repeat them as his words, and they were said before a king, so they will not be too broad words, nor too rude to speak before you) he said, "What, must I die? Send for a physician; wounds, sides, heart, must I die? Sounds, sides, heart, must I die?" And thus he went on, and there could be nothing gotten from him but "wounds, sides, heart, must I die? Must I die, and go from all these?"

Here is all; here is the end of the man who makes his

portion to be in this world. Another rich man who lives not far from the place that I myself lived in heretofore, when he heard his sickness was deadly, sent for his bags of money and hugged them in his arms, saying, "Oh, must I leave you? Oh, must I leave you?" And another who, when he lay upon his sick bed, called for his bags, laid a bag of gold to his heart, and then bid them take it away, saying, "It will not do, it will not do." Another, when he lay upon his sickbed, his friends came to him and said, "What do you lack? What would you have? Would you have any beer? Do you want you anything?" "Oh, no," said he. "I want only one thing, peace of conscience; that I would have. It is not beer, friends, or an easy pillow I want, but ease of conscience." Oh, consider now whether there is not likely to be perplexity in your spirits?

(2) You must be called to an account for all, though (as I told you before) not to account for the right to use, but not for right using. And do but now think with yourselves, if you now have so much as you cannot reckon, how then will you be able to reckon for it if you cannot now reckon it? Now you have so much that you cannot count; how will you be able to give an account of what you have now, especially when you have had no thoughts of this before?

(3) There is at last a dreadful portion indeed at the day of judgment. Oh, the shame and confusion that will be upon the faces of the men of the world, especially when they shall see, perhaps, their poor neighbors having their portion with Christ in glory! Perhaps a poor boy, a poor servant in the house, is advanced to glory, and they themselves are standing on the left hand to be cast out. Perhaps some of these poor hospital boys shall be admitted to eternal glory while some of you who are their great masters shall be cast out eternally. And what an infinite shame and confusion would this be to you? Oh, now I see what it is to trust in God and not to trust in Him! These

are happy who would trust for the future, but I am miserable who dared not trust in Him. And then what will the conclusion be? Psalm 11:6 says that the Lord will "rain snares and fire and brimstone . . . and this shall be the portion of their cup." Here is the portion of the ungodly at last. And Matthew 24:51: "Appoint him his portion with the hypocrites; there shall be weeping and gnashing of teeth." That is the portion of hypocrites in the conclusion.

Now here you see the end of all. What do you think then of your portion now? Think but of one text and I will be done with this. Job 27:8: "What is the hope of the hypocrite though he hath gained, when God taketh away his soul?" Mark, there were many hypocrites who aimed to get in the world, and cannot get in the world, God crosses them here. Well, but suppose you aim at gain, and can get what you would have; you have gotten all you would desire, but what hope has a hypocrite though he has gained, though he has grown never so rich and gotten all he desires, when God takes away his soul? His time is coming; it will be ere long, and it may be ere long the portion of some who are here present.

Perhaps this text of mine may then ring in their ears when they lie upon their sick beds, perhaps within a month or six weeks, or a quarter of a year, when God's time shall be, and then conscience may repeat this sermon in your ears. "I heard one day that there was a generation of men that have their portion in this world, and now I am afraid I am one of them. There is an end of my portion; only I must go to my other portion." That will be very dreadful. But I must not make an end till I speak something of the next point. I shall leave the point very bare.

PARTICULAR 5. Who is the man who has his portion in this world? It is a poor portion, as I have set it out to you, but every one will go away and say, "I hope it is not I. I hope it is not I. I hope God has a better portion for me than this!"

Therefore give me leave to speak in the name of God to you, and I'll only speak from God, and out of His Word to you, to point out the man and woman who is likely to have their portion here, living and dying in such a condition. I now am speaking of that man who is in such a condition. I shall open to you that, in his present condition, the Lord pronounces this day that his portion is in this world. Who is he?

He is that man to whom God gives in this life nothing but what belongs to this life; that is the man apparently. If God gives you your estate, and if He does not give you something besides your estate, a principle that is a seed of eternal life in you here in this world, certainly He never intends good to you in the world to come. There are many men who have a great deal in this world, and they say, they hope God will be merciful to them in the world to come. Now this is a certain truth: That man to whom God denies spiritual mercy in this world, God will deny eternal mercy to in the world to come. This therefore should be your care: "Does God increase my estate in this world? Oh, that the Lord would give a proportionate measure of grace too, else it is nothing! Lord, you give me here a great estate; if Thou givest not to me grace with it, a proportionate measure of grace to use to Thy glory, I would have been better off without this." Is this your care? I put it to your conscience. As your estate increases, are you solicitous at the throne of grace that the Lord would give you a proportionate measure of grace to manage your estate for His glory? Then peace be to you; you are not the man.

And then further you may examine it by the workings of your hearts about your present portions:

1. Do you enjoy what you have for itself, and do your hearts terminate on what you enjoy. One who is godly and has his portion beyond these things enjoys the creature, aye, but it is God in it that he enjoys. It is sweet to him that he can feel and taste the love of God in it. Aye, but a car-

nal heart enjoys the creatures, runs away and is terminated there. He looks at the creature, but little at God. Divers of your hospital children look more at the men who were their friends to bring them into the hospital when they were fatherless and motherless and shiftless than they look at the founders of the hospital. They little think to thank God for them, but if they meet with him who was the one to bring them in, they will thank him for his kindness.

So it is with men: They look at the creature who was the means of bringing them in, but a godly heart looks at the root of all. I remember it is said of one who came into the treasures of Venice that he saw tables of gold and silver there. He pointed down and looked at the bottom of the table, and one asked him, "Why is your eye so at the bottom?"

"Oh," said he, "I am looking at the root of all this."

Oh, alas! It is a small matter for a man who has a great trade to have a great portion. So many men look not so much at the root, whereas a godly man, though he has but a little, yet he looks at the root, at the love of God and the covenant of grace. That is the root of all, and this is the thing that satisfies his heart. When a man takes a potion, medicine, he often puts it into his milk. Now the milk is not the thing that makes the medicine work, but it is the medicine in it. So it is the goodness of God that satisfies a gracious heart and not the creature that is operative so much upon a gracious heart.

2. You may examine how your hearts are set upon these things of the world by whether your hearts go out with full strength to them. If you make your bellies to be your god, then your end will be destruction (as the apostle says). If the things of the earth are a gulf to swallow your heart up, there is another to swallow you up hereafter.

3. Ask yourself how the loss of the things of the world take your heart. Do you not count yourself an undone

man when you have lost some comforts? Do you not come home to your wife and children and say, "I am an undone man?" Why? What's the matter? "I have lost some part of my estate!"

Oh, carnal heart! One who is gracious may have some crosses, but no losses at all because he enjoys all in God. He has God to make up all his losses. And, the truth is, if you were truly godly, whatever afflictions you meet with (as we say a man may put all in his eye, so you may, if you are godly, put all your crosses in your eyes), you are so far from being undone.

4. Further examine whether these things of the world are not the only suitable things to your hearts, whether you bless not yourselves in these as in your happiness. Ivy will clasp about a rotten tree, and cannot be taken off it without tearing. And the heart of a worldling will clasp about these rotten comforts as the only agreeable thing. You may hear them sometimes tell with joy that "we were in such a place, and we were so merry, and had the bravest meeting." Oh, what was there? "Why, there was singing, roaring, and blaspheming the name of God; and yet it was the bravest meeting that could be." When did you ever come from an ordinance of God and say, "to my heart this day." Did you ever go from the Word with as merry a heart, and rejoice for it among your friends, as you did from a merry meeting? You may fear you are the man who has your portion here.

And then this is more clear for every one to examine his heart in, and if I were to give but any one evidence whether a man has grace or not I would give this as much as any one. A man who has some estate in the world, put this to him:

5. What do you account to be the chief good of your estate more than you had before, or more than another man has? A man who has gotten an estate more than he had, or more than his brother, there are many things in

his estate that he will think good. "Now I may live in better fashion than I could before; now I may have more freedom than I had before; now I may have more credit in the world than I had before; now I may have my own mind, and satisfy my own lusts more than I had before, or that another man can do." Is this not the thing you most rejoice in? Yea, is it not true that some of your hearts, if they were ripped up, this would be the language of them, that you most rejoice in your estates, because by them you have fuel for your lusts? A poor man has not so much fuel for his uncleanness as you have, nor so much fuel for his lust of pride and malice as you have. And many rich men account the blessing, the good, and happiness of their estates to consist in this very thing: that now they may have a larger scope for their lusts than ever they could before. Alas, a poor man cannot go abroad and drink as you can do; a poor man cannot lay out so much money on a whore, an unclean wretch, as you can do—and you rejoice in this. And if this man has not his portion here, what man has? The Lord strike such a man's heart.

But on the other side, when God blesses a gracious heart in this world, though there is but a little grace, it will work this way: "The Lord has raised my condition above my brother, and therein the Lord gives me a larger opportunity to do Him service than my brother has, or than I had before. There is such a poor man; he is an honest man, but God knows he can do but little in the place where he is; he has but little means. But God has given me means, and this means enlarges my opportunity to do God service; and for this my soul blesses God. I count my estate happier in this , because I now may be of more use and do God more service than otherwise I could do." Have you such workings in your hearts, you rich men? If you have not, never be quiet till you get your hearts working in this manner. This will be a blessed testimony that God gives you a portion here, and intends another portion for you in the world hereafter.

6. What is that thing that you strive to make most sure? That which a man strives to make most sure is that in which he counts his happiness to consist. Oh, for your land and debts, you strive with all your might to make that sure; but as for the matter of your salvation and peace in Christ, you have a good hope in God, but take no pains to make it sure.

7. What do you admire most men for? Oh, such a man is happy! He has so much coming in, and has so much a year. But do you call the vile man happy? It is a sign that you have not had your eye enlightened by the Spirit of God. But now can you look upon even those who are poor and mean in this world, who have the least portion here, as most happy creatures because the Lord gives them the grace of His Spirit; and then, "Well, 'tis true, I have a greater estate than such a poor man who is my neighbor, or than such a poor man, but God knows he does God more service than I do. He prays more, and more heartily in one day than I do in a whole year. Oh, the Lord has other manner of prayers and sighs come from his poor cottage than ever He had from my brave palace. I have my city house and country house, but they were never so perfumed with prayers. Some who live in poor cellars send up more prayers, and God has more honor from them than He has from me. In my family (perhaps) there is cursing and blaspheming of God; in such poor cottages there is (perhaps) blessing and praising of God." Now see if you look upon them as the most happy people in the world.

8. What are you careful to lay up for your children? That is likely to be your portion. If the things of the world take up your care for your children most, that is an argument that you think your children have a good portion. If you can leave them so many thousands, it is likely that it is your portion too if you count it theirs.

9. Examine what your services are:

Do you put off God with slight services? Then know your portion is likely to be of God's slight mercies.

Are you hypocritical in your service? Do you aim at the praise of men in outward duties? That is a sign you have your reward here.

Are your services forced? Are you compelled in your services? Is it merely conscience that compels you, and not an inward agreeableness between the frame of your heart and holy things? Then it's likely a servant's portion is yours, and not a child's portion.

10. Further, have you heretofore been a forward professor in religion, and have you forsaken the ways of God? I'll give you a dreadful Scripture for this. Jeremiah 17:13: "All that forsake Thee shall be ashamed, and they that depart from Me shall be written in the earth." All that depart from God shall be written in the earth. If you have been forward heretofore, and now come to be more ancient, if you are dead, dull, and careless, here is a text for you. Go home and tremble lest you are a man whose name is written in the earth.

11. Does not God, for the present, curse your portion? You find the more you have, the worse you grow. It is as if a man should eat meat at someone's table, and as soon as he has eaten it begins to swell, he will conclude that certainly the meat was poisoned. So when your estate rises, your heart rises with pride; surely it was poisoned with the curse of God that was on it.

12. Examine your heart by this, whether God has convinced you, so that it stops the great current of His mercy I spoke of. The soul that has its portion in this world looks no further but to God's general bounty, and looks not to what stops the great current of God's grace. He is not brought to be sensible of his need of Christ, and of His satisfaction unto divine justice; but now the heart God intends eternal good to, such a heart the Lord causes to understand that there is such an infinite breach between

God and it cannot be made up but by the mediation of the Son of God. That heart says, "Therefore, Lord, it is not in any righteousness of mine, nor in anything that any creature in heaven and earth can do, that I expect to have my portion from, but in the mediation of the Son of God. That I look after, and my heart closes with that mediation. I look upon that as the spring of all my worth." He is a man indeed who is not likely to have his portion in this world.

13. The man who spends his days without having some fear, lest God should put him off with the things of this world, there may be some danger of that. In Jude 12, it is said of some that they fed themselves without fear. You can go now to a merry meeting, and can go and feed upon the cheer; you eat without fear, and never have such a thought in your heart as this: "What if God should put me off with these things? I hear indeed there are some men who are put off so; what if it should prove to be my portion? What a miserable creature would I be?" I fear there are some men who never had such a thought in their lives. The wicked are described as men who eat without fear.

PARTICULAR 6. Let me give this exhortation to you, and then be done. This exhortation must be divided, first, unto you who have some evidences that God has given you a better portion, that God has not put you off with the portion of this world.

1. Oh, bless the Lord for his goodness to you! "The Lord He hath shewed you better things than these are; your line is fallen into a good ground, you have a goodly inheritance." When David looked at the prosperity of wicked men, his conclusion is, in Psalm 73:13: "I have cleansed my heart in vain, and washed my hands in innocency," but, in verse 24, "guide me with Thy counsel, and afterward receive me to Thy glory."

2. Be content with your portion here; do not murmur

and repine, for though you have not so much as others have yet you have what will make you happy forever. Remember that Jerome, in one of his epistles, tells of one Dydimus, who was a learned, godly preacher, but blind. Alexander came to him, and, meeting him, asked him, "What, are you not troubled for want of sight?" And he indeed confessed, it was a very sore affliction to him. Then Alexander began to chide him, "What, has God given you the excellency of an apostle, of a minister of Christ, and are you troubled for want of your sight, of that which mice and rats may have? Are you troubled at that, and rather not taught to bless God who has given you so great a mercy as to make you such an instrument of His service?" So may I say to you who are godly, has God given you Jesus Christ? Has He given you Himself to be your portion? And are you troubled that you have no more of what beasts may have as well as yourselves? Oh, be ashamed of any mournful discontentments for want of the comforts of this world!

3. Do not envy any wicked men for their portion. I remember a story I have heard of a poor soldier who was condemned to die merely for taking a bunch of grapes from a vine; for there was a strict law that whoever should take any thing from that place they went through should die for it. He had taken a bunch of grapes, and he was condemned to die. And as he went to his execution, he went eating the grapes. Someone came to him and said, "You should think of something else," to which he answered, "I beseech you, sir, do not envy me my grapes; they have cost me dearly." So may I say of all the men of the world, we have no need to envy them for anything they have; it will cost them very dearly.

4. Do you live like such as God has not put off with the portion of this world? Manifest in your conversations that you look for higher and better things than the things of this world; show they are but slight in your eyes. Zebulun

and Naphtali jeopardized their lives; they looked upon their lives as little worth for that cause. So look upon your estates as despicable; be willing to improve them all for public good, in a public cause, yea, be willing to jeopardize not only your estates, but your names, your liberties, and your lives. And those who shall do so, those whom God has given hearts to do so among you, perhaps some of you may look upon them as men in a sad condition, "Oh, such a man in such a place is looked upon, and he is likely to be undone; if not his life is in danger." But such a one who shall, out of a good principle, be willing to venture his life and estate, and appear in a good cause, that man should be most honored, and looked upon as the most happy man of all. And indeed herein he shows himself to be a man who looks for a higher portion than these things here, as those in Hebrews 11:14: "For they that say such things declare plainly that they seek a country."

So you see men who might live as comfortably for outward things as you, and (did their consciences give way) they could be as quiet as you; but conscience puts them upon it that, seeing God calls them to a public place, they should be content to put all at God's feet. Though you may think it hard, and they are in most danger, they show plainly they are men of another country and should be most honored.

Take but this principle with you: The more any one gives up his estate, the more comfort he has in his estate, whether in the enjoyment of it or in the loss of it. Express it thus: When one resigns all that he has—estate, liberty, name, life—to God, the more often it comes into God's hands, the better it comes when God gives him them again. A carnal heart, when once he has these things, will not trust God with them, but will have them at his own keeping. But now a gracious heart, though he has all these from God, yet every day he is willing to give up all to God, and to trust God with them again. Though he is a rich man, he is willing every day to come and beg his bread at his father's gates, and give up all. Now he gives up all in the truth of his heart to God, and God gives him it all again. So long as in a lawful way he enjoys it, he has it afresh from God.

Now this I say, the more often anything comes out of God's hand, the sweeter and better it is. Wicked men's estates come but once out of God's hands, and therefore there is not so much comfort in them; but a godly man's estate comes a hundred times from God, for every resignation gives it to God, and God gives it to him again. Therein is comfort! And, oh, blessed are they who live so as to declare they look for another country, and that their portion is not here! Let the men of the world think them foolish to venture themselves so. God and His saints have declared that their portion is not here.

This word of exhortation from God is, second, that every one in this place would yet put on to make more sure of another portion besides the portion here in this world. Put on, why?

First, you are all made capable of higher and better things, than the things of the world are. There is no one here but has an immortal soul, and therefore is capable of communion with Father, Son, and Holy Ghost; and that is another manner of business than to eat, drink, and have pleasure with the flesh here awhile. Has God made your natures capable of such glory? Do not debate yourselves, and that humanity God has put into you, to satisfy yourselves with husks when there is meat enough in your Father's house. He may be your Father for all I know, and therefore put on.

Second, let the poorest sort put on who have but a little portion here, yet there is as fair way for you to have the God of heaven and earth to be your portion, to have whatever Jesus Christ has purchased by His blood to be your portion, to have heaven, eternity, and immortality to be your portion (I say). There is as fair a way for it as for the greatest prince in the earth; you may come to have a portion. Here indeed a man, a poor apprentice, may say, "My father is dead and has left me no portion." Aye, but you who are poor apprentices, and others, and the poor hospital boys who live upon charity, it's possible some poor wretches there may come to have their portion in God, Christ, and immortality, as well as the greatest and richest of all. Therefore raise up your hearts here, you who are the poorest and meanest, and know you are born for high things.

If I should come and tell one who is a poor boy in a blue coat, "Now, whatever you are, a rich man will adopt you to be his child and make you his heir," that would raise up his heart. Well, however meanly you live now, you may be a glorious creature hereafter, if so be you have a heart to put upon it and seek after your portion. Then you'll say, "Lord, what should we do that our portion should be a higher portion than in this world?" The first thing I would put you upon is this:

(1) Let the whole course of your life be steered (as it were) with the fear of God, lest this should be all that you have. As it was a sign before, so now I may make use of it as a means. Let your course of life be steered (as it were) with the fear of God lest that God with this should put you off. Hold forth this in every action, that any one may say by your conversation, "Surely this man, this woman, has some fears lest God should put them off with a portion in this world."

And this especially applies to you who have great portions in this life, and know you have done God little service. You know that there are many poor people who live upon alms and have done God more service than you— you have most cause to fear. Those who are rulers and governors have most cause to fear, unless they have mighty good evidence in their hearts: Chrysostom, upon

Hebrews 13, speaking of those who are governors, said, "I wonder that any governor should be saved." I will not say so, but he said so; there is a great deal of hazard. Christ tells us, too, that a man who has a great portion in this world, though it's possible he may have more hereafter, yet it is doubtful.

It is the counsel of one to a king of Portugal, "I desire you to grant me this favor, that every day you would but think of this text, 'What profits it a man, if he should gain the whole world, and lose his own soul?' Spend some time every day to think of this text, and pray to God that He would give you the true understanding and sense, that God would show you what there is in this text." The same counsel I give to you: Daily pray to God to make you understand what there is in this text, that there are men who have their portion in this world.

(2) Labor to take your hearts off from all these outward comforts that are here. Take your spirits off. "He that will be rich shall fall into many temptations." Know it is not necessary (so you should conclude, everyone in your own hearts) that you should have an estate in this world, but it is necessary you should make your peace with God. It is necessary that you should provide for your soul, but as far as how things are with you here, there is no great necessity.

(3) Set the glory of heaven and eternity daily before your eyes, and be trading for higher things than these are. You who are great merchants, you are trading for thousands, while many poor people now who go up and down in the streets, and cry some mean thing, think well if they can get eighteen pence in a whole day carrying things upon their heads and crying in the streets. But a rich merchant can go out in the morning and make a bargain, and perhaps get five hundred pounds in an hour. So the men of this world are like poor women who go with things upon their heads and get eighteen pence in a day; but a

godly man has communion with God, and in a quarter of an hour gets what he would not lose for hundreds or for thousands.

It was a speech of Cleopatra to Anthony, "Why, Anthony you are not to fish for gudgeons and trouts, but you are to angle for castles, towers, forts, and cities. You are to fish for them!" So may I say, if you have an immortal soul within you, you are not so much to angle to make provision for the flesh, for meat, drink, and clothes, but for heaven and immortality. Set those continually before your eyes.

(4) Honor God with your substance here; lay out your portion here for God. And, oh, that I could but convince you of one more principle of divinity, and that is this: There is more excellency and good in one virtuous action than there is in all the creatures in heaven and earth (except for the works of angels and others of the saints). Take all creatures, sun, moon, stars, seas, earth, all the riches in the world, pearls, put all together, yet this is the true divinity, that there is more excellency in one virtuous action than there is if you had all these things to be your possession. If men were convinced of this, they would be abundant in good works then.

You think it a brave thing if you have so much coming in for the year. Do but one good action for God out of an upright principle, and there is more excellency in that one action than there is in your estate if you had ten thousand times more added to it. Certainly this will make those who are rich to be rich in good works. The Scripture says, "Charge them that are rich in this world, that they be rich in good works." There is a richness in good works, as well as in an estate. Oh, improve, lay out your estate for God.

I remember Ambrose, in his sermons upon the rich man, said, "It is not more honor that so many children shall ask of you as their father, than that so many pieces of gold shall call you their lord?" These pieces of gold (as it were) call you lord, and there are two or three children shall call you father; is there not more excellency to have a couple of poor orphans, while you are alive in this world, call you father than to have so many bags of gold call you master? Oh, therefore lay out your portion; give a portion to six and seven. In 2 Corinthians 9:8, the apostle prays for the Corinthians, that God would make them abundant in all grace, that He would fill them with grace so that they might abound in all sufficiency. But what for? Verse 11: "Being enriched in every thing to all bountifulness"; and then, verse 12, "for the administration of this service," that you may be enriched in all bountifulness. What for? "for the administration of this service." Now the words in the Greek are "for the administration of this liturgy." So the words in the Greek are, "that you may abound, and have all grace to abound in the administration of this liturgy."

My brethren, oh, how happy it would be if men were plentiful in this divine service that I am speaking of, and well versed in this liturgy. The apostle calls bounty a "liturgy." That service of God that is divine service indeed is a happy liturgy to be well-versed in.

(5) If you would not be put off with this portion in the world, be sure that all the services you perform to God are choice services. You expect choice mercies, so let your services be choice services. Be sure your works are supernatural works. You'll say, "How shall I know that?" If I had time I could make it out clearly to you, but know this, a supernatural work is that which has a supernatural principle, aims at a supernatural end, and is done in a supernatural manner. What makes it a supernatural principle is that it is grace that makes it suitable to my heart, and not only that I do it out of conviction of conscience. What makes it a supernatural end is that I aim at God and not at myself.

You shall know a natural affection by this: If it is kept within bounds it is natural; if it is out of bounds it is not natural. I'll make use of it in another way. When you come to the service of God, if you think to limit God in His service, this is but a natural service. You'll go so far and there stop. But if it is a supernatural service, you'll let out your hearts (if it were possible) infinitely to God. You cannot be infinite, that's true, but you'll propound no bounds (no limits to your service); and this is indeed the truth of grace, when it has the impression of God's infiniteness upon it. God's infiniteness is that whereby He is without all limits. So, where God sets no limits, there the soul is without all limits and bounds in the way of grace, that is, desires to answer God (if it were possible) by an infinite way; these are supernatural works.

(6) And then, would you not have your portion in this world, and be willing to cast away whatever of your portion you have gotten sinfully. Aye, in the name of God charge this as a special thing to take home with you: Whatsoever man or woman in this place would not have his portion in this world, but would have his portion in the world to come, whatsoever of his portion he has gotten in a sinful way, cast it away presently; never sleep with it; lie not down one night with it. That's an old rule, but a true one. All the repentance you have in the world, and all your sorrowing for your sin, will never obtain pardon without restitution if you be able. Unless you do what you are able to restore, you can never have comfort or the pardon of that sin. If you have gotten it when you were young apprentices, first set up a way with it, else it will spoil all. You'll never have any other portion from God,

These hands of mine once had that given to them to be a means to convey, to restore what was gotten wrongfully. The wrong was done fifty years ago, and after fifty years the conscience of the man troubles him, and he comes to restore that wrong, and desires it may be conveyed to such a place where he had done wrong. Know therefore that all the sweet morsels that any time you have so delightfully gotten down must come up again, and therefore willingly let them go up. Resolve before you go out of this place that whatever you have gotten wrongfully, you will never keep it against your will. Do it willingly, else you cannot have any comfort in the portion you have, nor have any portion in the world to come.

If there is any true divinity in the world, this is true divinity; and yet it is hard to convince any covetous men who have gotten much this way, things entrusted to them, such as those who are masters of hospitals. Be sure you do not keep that, aye, for certainly you'll curse the time you ever took it. And therefore let the charge of God be strong upon you this day to cast out whatsoever you have gotten falsely.

I read a story of one who, upon a time, hearing that place of Scripture, in Isaiah 5:8 read, "Woe to them that join house to house." He burst out into a loud cry, "If woe be to them that join house to house, then woe to me and my children." So upon what you have heard this day, there is a company that shall have their portion in this world, and especially those who will keep anything they have wrongfully gotten; many may have cause to say, "Woe to us, then, and unto our children."

(7) Be willing to join with those who have suffered for God. If you would have your portion in another life, be willing to join with the sufferers for Christ. So Moses did: Though he was in the way to preferment, yet he chose rather to suffer affliction with the people of God than to enjoy the pleasures of sin for a season. Join rather with them than with jolly blades of the world. It is safer to join with the sufferers than to join with those who are the jolly and brave spirits.

And so I have done, only desiring that the Lord would settle all home upon your spirits. If so be because something may or may not be so pleasing to the palate of everyone as some other, but if for that you should reject what has been said, and go away and slight this Word of God, know that this text one day may prove to be as scalding lead in your consciences. And what is said of that one in Psalm 52:7 may prove to be your portion: "This is the man that made not God his strength, but trusted in the abundance of his riches."

"This is the man." So you may be pointed out one day, Doeg was a great courtier, and because he was an officer of King Saul's, and because he had his favor, he trusted in the favor of the king and in his riches. And what did he care for David? Yea, by the text it appears he was one who made some show of religion too. 1 Samuel 21:7: "He was detained before the Lord." Tremelius thinks it was either out of some religious vow, or to keep the Sabbath, or something concerning the Law, that he was detained before the Lord; yet he was a vile malignant against David, and all because he trusted in the great countenance he had at court.

Now this is the man who did not make God his trust, but who trusted in his great riches. The Lord forbid this Scripture should be made true of any of you.

I leave this text with you who are rich men. Take heed that you do not trust in your great riches.

I leave this text with you who are in places of dignity and honor. Take heed that you do not have your portion in this world.

I leave this text with voluptuous men, given up to your pleasures. Take heed that you do not hear this one day: "Son, remember, in your lifetime you had your pleasure."

I leave this text with those who dare not trust God for a portion to come.

Above all I leave this text with all hypocrites. Let them take heed it is not said to them, "Here is your reward."

Consider what has been said, and may the Lord give you understanding in all things.